PRAYERS
IN
COMMUNITY

Thierry Maertens
Marguerite DeBilde

Fides Publishers Inc.
Notre Dame, Indiana

PRAYERS IN COMMUNITY

Thierry Maertens

Marguerite DeBilde

Fides Publishers Inc.

Notre Dame, Indiana

TRANSLATED BY JEROME J. DuCHARME

Contemporary Prayer WAS PUBLISHED ORIGINALLY IN FRENCH UNDER THE TITLE Livre de la Priere, COPYRIGHT, EDITIONS CENTURION, PARIS.

ISBN: 0-8190-0446-4

© COPYRIGHT: 1974, FIDES PUBLISHERS, INC.
NOTRE DAME, INDIANA

NIHIL OBSTAT: CHARLES EHLINGER
PARIS, SEPTEMBER, 1969

IMPRIMATUR: E. BERRAR
PARIS, SEPTEMBER, 1969

contents

Indexes (In Volume II)

foreword

Give us a prayer of our very own!

One day the disciples asked Christ to teach them a prayer which would be their very own (Luke 11:1). He began to teach them to pray the "Our Father." It is this same on-going challenge for each generation and each believer in the Church to learn to adore the Father in spirit and truth (John 4:24). Today's liturgical renewal as experienced in small worshiping groups and in the privacy of searching individuals testifies to this effort and desire. It is always necessary for us to relearn how we are to pray the Our Father and to make that prayer relevant to our vocabulary and sensitivities. Our prayer must reflect the hopes and uneasy moments of our often fragmented experience as men and Christians in today's world. The truth in these prayers opens us to change. We are then disposed to allow ourselves to be transformed by the evangelical force of this prayer.

This book gives witness to this kind of contemporary prayer. The authors and editors publish it knowing full well the limitations of the undertaking, but realizing also the necessity to take the initiative. These texts are presented to the reader as suggestions or sketches, rather than finished models or completed formulas. The prayers suggest diverse paths and themes. Various styles and types of prayer are tested. In this variety, however, there emerges a certain unity of spiritual universes from which the reader will sense familiar vibrations. Perhaps a resonant chord will not be struck.

It matters little in the long run whether these texts meet the reader's approval or disapproval. Their purpose is merely to stimulate each reader to participate according to his own prayer style in his creative experience of contemporary prayer, both personally and in community. If through agreement or opposition among individual Christians and communities there results a renewed desire to pray, then this book will have attained its purpose. It is not within the power of the authors to decide if this book will serve as a milestone in the effort to discover a contemporary liturgical prayer, fully faithful to the gospel, richly traditional and at the same time strongly reflecting the needs of modern man. But the authors hope they are not being presumptuous in expecting a certain degree of success.

These prayers are contemporary in the sense that their origin was marked by a very unique insertion into life. They have been formulated by believers guided by their lived experience or by groups and communities assembled to hear the Word of the gospel. The themes resound with the echo of modern situations and events. The clashes of today's struggles can also be heard. But here lies the limitation of the prayers and also their value. There was no forced attempt to "be modern." Being real was the only guideline. The reader will find religious vocabulary of yesterday mixed together with today's profane words. Biblical and liturgical tradition are translated into the language of the morning newspaper—as Karl Barth once said. Being faithful to the past and present has not always proven to be a happy marriage. Since we are now in an age of change, it is not easy to adapt yesterday's expressions to something that has meaning for us today. It is not easy to attain unity between tradition where our memory and our identity lie and the needs of modern times to which we are called upon to respond. Are these prayers for a generation of mutants? Described in this way, these prayers are even more relevant to us.

These prayers are grouped under two main headings: Prayers in Community and Prayers for Everyday Life. Although they are presented in separate volumes, the distinction is not easy to define. There are in a way two spheres. No doubt the distinction is explained by the fact of circumstances, persons, groups and temperaments. Nevertheless, there is a deeper, more fundamental meaning corresponding to the two streams in religious experience and probably even in human awareness.

1. First of all there is what can be called the sphere of the "sacred collectivity" or community. These are prayers for a group, community or congregation. Such prayers have a universal accent by embracing world history and salvation history and the scope of the limitless solidarities of modern man. The pulsations and tensions of life in the world seem to find synthesis in these thanksgivings, supplications and professions of faith. The man or the community which addresses God acts as spokesman for all humanity by personifying mankind in the different moments of the liturgical year. By reacting to the biblical word or to events, the community realizes that all humanity by being personified by Christ is involved in God's plan. The first volume of our book contains many unanswered questions at

the very moment when the liturgy itself demands flexibility. At times a more detailed explanation may seem in order. Paul Guérin has clarified some of those questions in the Afterword of Volume 1. He also gives some of his ideas on the characteristic signs of a modern community in prayer and hopes that some new eucharistic prayers might one day be created through this approach.

2. Volume 2, *Prayers for Everyday Life,* explores the interior shrines in the "sacred individual": "And when you pray, lock yourself in your room . . ." (Mt 6:6). It is paradoxical that today's men and women feel caught up in the enthusiasm and harassment of the relentless rhythm of modern living. For this reason they are well aware of boredom and new forms of anguish. Whatever mood prevails, each person needs now more than ever before to create an interior place where he is most truly himself. Retreating within himself, he confronts his lived experiences: his problems and discoveries; his situations of life, age and responsibility; his certainties and his doubts. It is within each human heart that the joys and difficulties of life form deep personal values. By getting beyond protests and confrontations and by taking off his masks, man enters into himself. Here we find unfolding the mystery of happiness and despair. Isn't it God who then has the opportunity to speak to us in order to interpret things clearly for us and fill us with the joy of being known and loved in the deepest part of our being? The Lord's beckonings to us are discovered in that secrecy where true decisions are made.

Here then is *Contemporary Prayer!* The last few pages contain a number of practical tables which can be useful in a variety of circumstances for community prayer and personal meditation. The authors, however, did not intend to exhaust all uses for this book. Together, the authors offer their endeavors and experiences to invite their brothers and sisters to deeper prayer.

prayers in community

introduction

In offering 73 prayer texts having literary themes and forms based on the liturgy, we do not intend them to be used interchangeably with official liturgical texts. Although the prayer of a local community should surely be acknowledged as the expression of the universal church, that characteristic does not rely on us alone. This concern that these are not official texts should not curtail experimentation. It is for this purpose that we present these prayers which make no pretense of going beyond the realm of private usage.

The reader will not find the precise rules of composition being closely followed. We have tested various modes of expression. The way these prayers are used will become more significant than the authors' original intent. Sometimes we use life to discover Christ. Sometimes we use scripture. Some prayers are quite lyrical and others are marked by a more somber, even colder, tone. Since the liturgy is now in a period of transition, it is necessary to open the greatest possible number of resources and then allow the people of God to adapt their prayers accordingly. These proposed texts lend themselves to a variety of creative uses.

It is evident that these texts have not been intended for use in every community. They are especially meant for home liturgies. If the scripture passages are read before the prayers, the homily or dialogue can be based appropriately on the themes in the prayer. These texts can also be helpful to private and family prayer. For the most part, we find prayers of thanksgiving, praise and penitential texts. In this respect, our work has important limitations: we invite the reader to join us in developing new formulas to express the meaning of the Lord's Prayer, the Kiss of Peace, Holy Communion and prayers which begin or end the liturgy.

The biggest difficulty to overcome has been to find an expression and vocabulary which permits modern man to find himself prayerfully before a God who no longer speaks primarily through nature and history. God is now more easily discovered in the human heart in terms of personal commitment and love. This is our first attempt at such a book, but we are certain that this experiment is worthwhile and will be shared by a great number of Christians.

1

This book is not completely original. An expression here and there will remind the reader of a modern song or of one of H. Oosterhuis' prayers which were the first in this field.

Generally speaking, the doctrinal inspiration comes from *The Guide for the Christian Assembly* (9 Volumes, Fides), the new commentaries on the lectionary.

doorman, who's in sight?

Mark 13:33-37
Agape/*Church; Doorman; Mansion.*

It is good indeed
to give you thanks,
Father of Jesus Christ,
for the dwelling place we build with you,
for the warmth within its walls
which rekindles our zeal;
for the well prepared table
where you share a meal with us;
for renewed acquaintances
and cherished friendships;
for the doorman who is in charge of the keys
not to keep the door closed
but to open it to all who come
until one day your Son will be among us;
for the house servants
with whom you entrusted
water for cleansing
and bread which strengthens,
wine which gladdens the heart
and words that give us courage!

People: O Lord, how can I recognize
the gifts you have bestowed upon me?
Each day I shall celebrate your great works.
Alleluia!

*   *   *

Look on, Jesus, the joyfilled spirit
of the household getting ready to receive you,
waiting for your knock which just now sounds at the door.
You confide in man
by giving house keys
to someone who cannot watch
even one hour with you.
You should know us better than
to choose household servants
from among people who dream

3

only of honors and high places.
And yet you have entrusted them with
the house of reunion, in your memory,
in a meal you intended
for all who dwell in your house
so that no one loses his way.

People: We proclaim your death, Lord Jesus,
we celebrate your resurrection,
we await your coming in glory.

*   *   *

Spirit of the Father and Son,
awaken the sluggish doorman
to the prestige of his role,
and nudge the servants caught up
in the frills of the world.
Inspire us with humility
when we begin concentrating too much
on serving ourselves.
Bring a serenity
to those who are tempted to quit their service
and desert the mansion.
Support the faithful servants who are selfless enough
to work toward making this
a more beautiful house, more worthy
of the stranger in search of a home,
through whom our Lord Jesus Christ
comes to us.

People: Through him, with him and in him,
all honor and glory
are yours, Father,
in the unity of the Holy Spirit,
for ever and ever. Amen.

the foreigner returns home by another road

Isaiah 60:1-6
Matthew 2:1-12

Examination of conscience/*Triumphalism; Institution;*
Centralization; Pride.

Before God
let us begin to question our attitudes and commitments
so that our city sets no other frontiers
except those of the universe.
Is it a pure and radiant appearance
which the Church presents to the world?
Does it invite people to encounter
Him whose glory the Church should be radiating?

People: In a Church which is being renewed,
        gather together, Lord,
        all men, our brothers.

We strive to make things rigid
in narrow frameworks and institutions.
But doesn't this degrade the silent mission
of the Servant who becomes flesh
in the ambiguity of our earthly condition?
Can men of today
still find God's love
in Christians who are spontaneous and loving?

People: In a Church which is being renewed,
        gather together, Lord,
        all men, our brothers.

We prefer organizations and centralized controls
which take credit for all human accomplishments.
Is this the way to respect
the rich diversity of each and every person?
Can men of today
still discover the fatherhood of God
in the mixed faces of his children?

People: In a Church which is being renewed,
        gather together, Lord,
        all men, our brothers.

We belong to the Church, light of nations.
Is this reason for pride,
or the source of responsibility and service?
Is there a need to strip ourselves
of racial or cultural privileges?
And what about the credit we take
for our generosity?
Can men of today
still discover
the generosity of God who loves them
as we forsake our superior attitudes?

People: In a Church which is being renewed,
                gather together, Lord,
                all men, our brothers.

*   *   *

We aspire to greater assurance and certainty,
and we are inflated by our own dogmas and wealth.
Don't we then become insensitive
to the treasures
which modern wisemen open before us?
Will we continue to demand
that they mold their discoveries
to our imperialistic drives?
Can men of today
still discover
through the opaqueness of our self-sufficiency
the God who welcomes each man as he is.

People: In a Church which is being renewed,
                gather together, Lord,
                all men, our brothers.

Isn't our mission in the world
too often degraded
by abusive propaganda
and aggressive triumphalism?
Do we readily examine
our work, our apostolate,
our religion, our holiness?
Can men of today
discover in the Church

the kingdom God prepares for them
if she fails to be the living sign of that kingdom?

People: In a Church which is being renewed,
           gather together, Lord,
           all men, our brothers.

at the end of a night with no dawn

Luke 21:25-36
Psalm 29
Matthew 26:36-46

Agape/*Destruction; Vigilance.*

You are the one who made the whole universe tremble;
you provoked the turmoil of the sea,
the tidal waves and the falling stars;
you just about scared to death
man trying to cope with his condition.

But today we defy your power.
Our explosions shake the universe,
and under the weight of our bombs
entire villages disappear,
more devastated than Jerusalem.

At the end of our night of suffering and anguish
dawn does not appear;
no light casts away the darkness of our fears.
Our faith demands an answer
and you seem deaf to those who search for you.

                    *   *   *

Do not tear us away from this turmoil
by unheard of prodigies.
Do not split the heavens for us
to restore a Jerusalem of peace and security.
Do not lift your Church higher than the people,
and do not dispense her from the trials of our times.
For you are not about to repair

with a simple wave of the hand
the cracks in our walls;
this was not your plan
when you had Jesus, your Son,
be born among us
to share our fear
and feel the risk of death and destruction.
He cried out with us in anguish;
he sweat his fearfulness in drops of blood;
he found himself alone,
forsaken by his Father.
He had nothing left in himself
except his courage to live and love;
he went beyond his own powers
to you, the source of his love.
That is why you raised him up
and he comes among us today
with great glory and power.
To have us share in his courage and glory,
he has set our table
with his bread and wine.
He taught us vigilance
and vigilance unveils for us the meaning of
the question which has no easy answer,
the event which defies logic,
the purposeless gesture,
the night without dawn.

*   *   *

Stir up, Lord, the vigilance of your Church,
so that she gives up trying to calm
the anguish of men
through false assurances;
Let her comfort troubled men
by proclaiming to them a Father
who welcomes them and loves them
as he has loved his Son
our Lord Jesus Christ.

leave and give escort

Isaiah 40:1-11   *Matthew 3:1-12*
Baruch 5:1-9   *Mark 1:1-8*
                     Luke 3:1-6

Eucharist/*Road*

Be praised, Father of Jesus Christ,
by all men, our brothers,
thrown, in search of you,
out on the roads of this world:
Abraham, the faithful wanderer;
Moses and his people in search of happiness
in the solitude of the desert;
the good Samaritan
discovering his neighbor on the road to Jericho.

People: Amen, Amen, Amen, Alleluia!

Be praised, Father,
by adventurers on the expressways
which trace the way to places where
men from all continents and worlds
come together to meet and share;
be praised
by engineers
who have cut down distances
by building better roads and vehicles.
Thanks to all of these people,
man becomes closer to man;
his misery is decried by everyone
and becomes intolerable;
his happiness too is ever more quickly given
to everyone to be shared.

People: Amen, Amen, Amen, Alleluia!

Be praised, Father,
by Jesus Christ, your Son,
who traveled down the road of men
by being entirely committed
to answer the needs of his brothers.
And when his road
became the way of the cross,

he gathered his companions for the last time
and sharing his viaticum with them
he gave you thanks.
Be praised, Father,
by all those who repeat the same action
around the same table,
in memory of your Son, Jesus Christ.

People: Amen, Amen, Amen, Alleluia!

4 And now, Father,
receive the sacrifices
which we attempt to make
as we follow the example of Christ.
We are trying to walk more energetically
in more brotherly companionship
as we make our long journey together.
Realize too that our highways
test our endurance,
and that there are no exit ramps.
And see the discouragement and exhaustion
of those who are stalled
at the side of the road.

People: Lord, the road is long
that leads to you!

omit Look at the life style
of those who make the road their profession:
mechanics and repairmen,
road workers and engineers,
drivers of tow trucks and trailer trucks;
Let your Spirit put new zest in their work
so that they are intent on serving others.

People: Lord, the road is long
that leads to you!

omit See that thirst for risk
in the hearts of astronauts
and explorers.
May their adventurous spirit
lead them eventually to you.

People: Lord, the road is long
that leads to you!

Accept the hesitations and uncertainties
of your Church;
be the shepherd of her shepherds;
do not allow even one sheep
to stray from your flock
as they make their way to your kingdom.

People: Lord, the road is long
              that leads to you!

And let all men of good will
find at the end of their quest for happiness
that they live and reign with you
together with the Son and Holy Spirit
for ever and ever.

People: Amen, Amen, Amen, Alleluia!

distress corrodes the heart

Baruch 5:1-9
Isaiah 40:1-11
Psalm/*Distress; Loneliness;*
              Jerusalem; City.

The exiles cried out to you in their distress
and the prophets consoled them;
they proclaimed to the exiles
a glorious Jerusalem
which would gather them together
in an endless life of happiness.
They preached about a road
leading to the fatherland
which fulfilled their dream.
But, at the end of the road,
why so many unfulfilled promises
and so many eccentric prophets?

*   *   *

So I cry out to God in my distress,
snatched away from my country, my neighborhood, my family,
a stranger in a land of plenty,
a dissatisfied misfit, ill-suited for work.

Which road will lead me back to Jerusalem?
Will anyone I know be at my doorstep to greet me?

I cry out to God in my distress.
Already my age is pulling me
out of the land of the living;
sickness flattens me in the corner of my room.
Which road will lead me back to Jerusalem?
And who will be there to greet me when I arrive?

I cry out to God in my distress,
an anonymous number in an assembly line,
voiceless in the decisions made by the power structure,
alienated from myself, my lover, my future.
Which road will lead me back to Jerusalem?
Who will be there to enroll me as a dignified and free citizen?

So I cry out to God in my distress.
I pay the highest price for my chance to live;
my skin is torn by shackles;
my future is blasted apart by explosions.
Which road will lead me back to Jerusalem?
And who will offer his life so that we have more peace and love?

And so I cry out to God in my distress,
thrown into an impersonal world,
battered and exiled,
restless and ignorant;
day after day I seek an escape.
Which road will lead me back to Jerusalem?
And which leader will restore righteousness?

* * *

Rejected by his own,
misunderstood by his friends,
forsaken by his Father,
even Jesus cried out to his Father in his distress.
He was dreaming of a Jerusalem
where he would assemble his brothers,
and in his imagination he pictured
a road which all men
would use to follow in his footsteps.

* * *

Give us, Lord, a new heart;
inspire generosity in us,

and the Jerusalem which your Son builds
will be even more beautiful;
let the construction stones be etched out
by the fiery chisel of love,
and tested by our fidelity.

impossible happiness

Isaiah 61:1-11   *1 Thessalonians 5:16-24*
Zephaniah 3:14-18   *Philippians 4:4-7*
Psalm/*Joy; Happiness; Celebration.*

You demand the impossible, Father,
in insisting we be joyful!
How will we smile
when we are hiding the child
who was born abnormal to us,
when we weep over
him (her) who shares our life?

People: How can we sing
        a song to the Lord
        in a foreign land?

How will we be joyful
when each day we hear the echo
of the cries of aborted babies
who are not given time to grow,
when each Sunday brings us before you
ashamed of our lack of concern.

People: How can we sing
        a song to the Lord
        in a foreign land?

How can we be joyful
when we doubt others
because we are filled with fear
as we fanatically defend
our prejudices and our habits?

People: How can we sing
        a song to the Lord
        in a foreign land?

How can we be joyful
when, out of disdain for men and their efforts,
we get inflated with false hopes
and count on miracles
to change the face of the earth?

People: How can we sing
a song to the Lord
in a foreign land?

*   *   *

We recall now
how your Son, Jesus Christ,
distributed bread and wine
and wished us the best:
may his joy be in us
and may our joy be complete.

People: Let my joy be in you
and may your joy be complete!

Joy of Jesus
who recognized himself as God's counterpart
in his earthly condition.
Joy of him who tasted the happiness of men
in taking on their flesh.

People: Let my joy be in you
and may your joy be complete!

Joy of an expanding brotherhood
formed around bread and wine;
joy tested by temptation
and made solid with God's help;
joy of taking a firm step forward
without turning around.

People: Let my joy be in you
and may your joy be complete!

*   *   *

Father, teach us how to celebrate;
be the animating force of our joy;
strengthen our faith in your presence;
activate our love and make it grow;
help us to respond to others.

Father, hasten that day
when weeping will cease
because we will have arrived
at the most beautiful of celebrations
in knowing and loving each man
for ever and ever.

People: Amen!

love and the child

Matthew 1:18-25
Luke 1:26-38

Prayers for special intentions/*Love; Celibacy; Child; Home*

Here we are, Father, in your presence,
and among us are our brothers and sisters
committed to voluntary celibacy,
who no longer find happiness in their choice.
Let this suffering not keep them distant from you
and let our acceptance and respect
sustain their faithfulness.

People: Be it done unto me, Lord,
according to your Word.

Here we are, Father, in your presence,
and among us are young people who envision
living celibacy in close union with you.
Let their witness bring new vigor to the witness we give
and help them find encouragement in our brotherhood.

People: Be it done unto me, Lord,
according to your Word.

Here we are, Father, in your presence,
and among us are responsible parents
who renew their love in childbearing.
Be present in their tenderness;
let their love bring into the world
some of the happiness
which each of us, because of Jesus Christ,
can offer to one other.

Here we are, Father, in your presence,
and among us are husbands and wives
who have decided to separate.
Let these broken families
which once received us,
as a witness to their union,
now find in our homes
comfort for their sorrows
and respect for their decision.
And let their uprooted children
share in the warmth of our friendship.

People: Be it done unto me, Lord,
according to your Word.

Here we are, Father, in your presence,
and among us are victims
of our erotic society.
Let husbands and wives be willing to
reach out to help engaged couples
as they grow toward a mature and generous love.

People: Be it done unto me, Lord,
according to your Word.

Here we are, Father, in your presence,
and among us are families
which had dreamed of bringing into the world
a happy child.
But their still-born or exceptional child,
their ungrateful or rebellious child
makes each day miserable.
We have no words
to console them and help them;
you alone, God, can speak to them;
ease up a little on their sorrow
so they will understand what you are saying to them.

People: Be it done unto me, Lord,
according to your Word.

Here we are, Father, in your presence,
and among us are people
fulfilled in their families,
happy in their celibacy.
Let their happiness be enchanting enough

to give rise to prayers of thanksgiving.
Let their happiness be tempered enough
to give support to those who are less happy.

People: Be it done unto to me, Lord,
           according to your Word.

christmas gifts from a generous god

Titus 3:4-7
Psalm/*Love; Gift.*

Gifts to be given and gifts to be received
distract us
and we forget about
the gift you gave us, Father,
in your Son, Jesus Christ.

A child has not always deserved
the gift his parents promise him.
But are we ever able to earn a gift?
You know what the answer is, Father;
you have given us everything in forgiving us.

Husbands and wives are about to exchange gifts
in simple gestures
in which the best of themselves can be found.
You give us another sign of your affection
in your gesture, Father,
which reconciles us to you and renews our hearts.

The lonely old man knows the sadness
of no longer offering any gifts;
the poor child is saddened by never receiving gifts.
The glitter of fancy shop windows is not for them.
Yet you, Father,
love as no one has ever loved;
you give yourself to the most distant person;
you offer yourself to the most isolated man.

The poor man offers his gift to his poor brother
in the poverty of a single package,
but richness is in his eyes
and what warmth in his heart!
Father, you also offer us at this table
a bread which takes away our selfishness.
You have shaped your Son's body
to be offered on the cross
and you have raised up his body

so that it becomes for us for all time
the grace of the present moment.

new life

Luke 2:1-14   *John 1:1-18*
Luke 2:15-20

Profession of faith/*Incarnation.*

I believe in a Father God,
whose word sustains men's lives
and the work of their hands in the universe.
For he is Life.

People: I believe in God the Father,
        creator of the universe.

I believe in his Son among us
who have been stumbling in darkness.
He was born among the very poor
to manifest God's grace.
For he is the Lord.

People: I believe in God's Son,
        born of a woman,
        who died and was raised up
        to deliver us from evil.

I believe in the Spirit
who makes us be born with God's life
and floods us with strength and energy
in our struggle to be faithful.
For he is Love.

People: I believe in the Holy Spirit
        who dwells in our hearts
        and renews our lives.

I believe in the Church
at the service of men
so that they may receive God's fullness.
For she is the messenger of the Good News.

People: I believe in the Church
        to which your Word is entrusted.

I believe in the new life
which bread and wine communicate
to God's witnesses in the world.
For this is our Glory.

People: I believe in life everlasting,
and I await the resurrection
in the hope of a new world
in which humanity finds its unity
in Christ our Lord.
Amen.

getting beyond our half truths

Luke 2:41-52
Agape/*Searching for God.*

It is right to give thanks
to Him who has arranged for all time
the earth and universe;
to Him who diffuses light
and fixes stars in the sky;
to Him who placed men at the heart of nature
to admire it and dominate it and make it more beautiful.

We can hardly call the creator by name
when so much evil and disorder reign in his work,
we can hardly call it providence
when complicated situations surround us.

But even beyond happiness and sorrow,
questions and answers,
beyond life and death,
you are our God,
and nothing can uproot us
from that deep part of our being
which is your love.

*   *   *

We call to mind
that you made yourself known
to the prophets of Israel

and to all those who have searched for you.
You are inaccessible and near,
mysterious and real,
unfathomable and familiar.
We recall that Mary and Joseph
knew you without understanding
even after three days of bewilderment and anguish,
three days of suffering and death.
We too should be about our Father's business;
to conquer our hesitancies and restlessness,
Jesus has broken the bread of wisdom for us.

*   *   *

Our faith is fragile, our commitments too measured,
and, nonetheless, here we are called to give witness.
Grant, Lord, that we become dissatisfied
with half truths and false securities;
don't let our responsibilities halt our searching,
never let us lose our modesty in our convictions,
so that by listening to each other
we might master the world
and make progress for mankind
in the spirit of love,
because this is our Father's business.

a time for building,
a time for tearing down

Ecclesiastes 3:1-9
Intercession/*Time; Eternity.*

This gathering around the eucharistic table
is for us a momentary pause
in time which speeds by
and no one can grasp.
Let us try to stop in space for an instant
and find God there and his eternity.

*   *   *

Time erases sorrows and joys,
the faces of the people we love,

our greatest undertakings.
Time devours everything it touches.
And too often we strive to rediscover time
through illusions and imagination,
through dreams and vain regrets,
or in the senseless agitation of activity.
Help us live in the eternity
which fills each present moment.
For God's Wisdom, which is above all things,
is in each of our actions,
and gives to the person who discovers it
the foretaste of God's eternity.

People: Lord, thy kingdom come.

Time passes by its very nature;
but we don't know how to pass time
and we cannot stretch time
by jetting across time zones.
We don't have time for what is essential;
we kill time and lose time in futile endeavors.
Nevertheless, the fullness of time has begun
when a man born like us from a woman
contemplated eternity in each hour of his life,
when he offered his followers
bread and wine, imperishable food,
when he seized the instant of his death
in order to place his entire being
under the gaze of eternity.
Help us find the time
to break away from brutal and rapid events
as we give ear
to God's Word about each of these events.

People: Lord, thy kingdom come.

Time does not go in reverse;
time is not an endless cycle,
an absurd or monotonous repetition;
it runs toward a hidden reality.
It's our fault that we keep preoccupied with time,
but we habitually conserve peripheral issues,
habits and judgments, institutions and customs.
Confusing the immobile with the eternal,

we show to the world the face
of a Church which is becoming outdated.
The Word became flesh in human time,
not to stop time,
but to give it meaning with his vibrant eternity.
Grant that we learn to accept
reforms and transitions,
delays and postponements,
advances and setbacks;
And amid all these changes, open our hearts
to welcome the eternal value
of each moment which is offered to us.

People: Lord, thy kingdom come.

in the light of the star

Matthew 2:1-12

Acclamations/*Encounter; Universalism.*

We give thanks to you, Father,
for the secret desire in every man's heart
to encounter his brothers and live with them
in sharing riches
and exchanging cultures;
for it is in so doing that man is made
in your image and likeness.

People: Glory to you, Lord!

We give thanks to you, Jesus Christ;
you have given up your privileges as God's Son,
your rights as Abraham's son,
and even your human life itself;
for you have fully grasped the human condition
and readied yourself for all encounters!

People: Glory to you, Lord!

We give thanks to you, Holy Spirit;
you bring about our communication with one another
so that we no longer know what it means to be contemporary;
for in you, Holy Spirit, each person is known;

the stranger becomes the host;
the pagan becomes a brother;
the adversary turns into a close friend
and each person becomes intimate with God.

People: Glory to you, Lord!

from the top
of the pinnacle

Matthew 4:1-11   *Mark 1:12-15*   *Luke 4:1-13*

Eucharist/*Temptation; Power; Desert.*

Father,
you have given to man your own life
so that he might discover in himself
your reflection and image,
so that in everything he seeks to know
your will.

We thank you
for Jesus Christ, our Lord,
the first among men
in whom your resemblance
has been kept faithful and perfect.

This is the reason why he refused
to perform the miracle
which would have brought him power and glory.
He remained faithful to his human condition
and to the death which fulfilled his life;
he resisted all temptations
to make himself like God.

That is why, Father,
you have glorified him
and have given him in full measure
that divine life
which he expected from you alone.
We also are walking down here
in his footsteps;
we proclaim your love for Jesus
and, with all those who hear his word,
we sing:

People: Amen! The Lord is holy!
          God of the universe,
          heaven and earth are filled with your glory!

*   *   *

Be mindful that your church and her members
are still in the desert
of trial and temptation.
They sometimes falter
and are tempted to exercise influence
with their resources of wealth.
They forget their earthly condition
by appealing to absolutes
in their disciplinary laws and doctrines.
They continue to make friends
with the satisfied and powerful
and abandon the weak and oppressed.

In your name, Lord,
we offer to you today
their longing for conversion
and their desire to be faithful.

We wish to cleanse your people
of our desire for clannishness and power,
and our preference for comfort and security.
Father, make our attitude agreeable to you;
we express our intention here in this meal of brotherhood
which Jesus blessed as a sign of how he conquered
temptation and himself.

People: Through him, with him and in him
all honor and glory
are yours, Father,
in the unity of the Holy Spirit,
for ever and ever.
Amen.

alone again!

Genesis 2:7-3:7   *Luke 4:1-13*
1 Corinthians 10:1-12
Penitential Prayer/*Confusion; Desert; Temptation.*

We are not far from thinking,
Father,
that we are stronger than your Son

and are able to expose ourselves to the danger
of falling into every temptation.

We have tasted the fruit of the tree of knowledge
and our laws clearly discern good from evil;
we no longer have to pay attention to
the hesitations of our consciences.

We spend our money lavishly
on insurance premiums and investments
and thereby entertain the illusion
that new angels will wisk us away,
under the protection of their wings,
beyond tomorrow, beyond eternity.

We establish anonymity
in our towns and cities,
and the level of our advertising,
our propaganda, and our customs
makes us fall down in adoration
before the very gods of affluence.

By being rich, we have sold our own freedom
along with the freedom of the very poor,
in order not to feel guilty;
we have divinized our quest for the good life
to justify our choices
which we never bother to reevaluate.
And here we are once again in the desert;
our idols of blood and neon lights
will crumble away, sooner or later,
as does everything which is inane;
our human condition
remains confusing, despite our alibis,
and we have to grasp life with both hands
in the hope of becoming sane.

*   *   *

We give you thanks,
Father of Jesus Christ,
for the presence of your Son
in this earthly life.
He shared our thirst for security;
he sought out needed certitudes;
but, faithful to his condition as man,

he did not cling to the narrow hopes of one nation;
he did not claim false divinizations.
He seized life as it is,
stamped with the death he freely accepted,
having no other assurance
except the confidence he had in you.

We proclaim his death
and we partake in it through his bread and wine.
Have your Spirit keep us in solitude
where encounter with you is possible,
so that our faithfulness and brotherhood
with every man become more alive.

heaven is not reserved just for sad people

Matthew 17:1-8   *Luke 9:28-36*
Mark 9:1-8

Agape/*Change; Brotherhood; Communion.*

What happiness we have here, Father;
your Son is in our midst.
our words, our hopes,
our friendships, our works,
everything is changed when he is here,
like the sun dissipates
the mist in our valleys.
We don't have to climb mountains
to discover your presence
because your face is man's face.

People: We are really happy to be here, Father;
           your Son is in our midst.

What happiness we have here, Father;
your Son is in our midst.
We spend our time trying with our hands
to empty the sea
which slips back again through our fingers;
but everything is changed when he is here,

like a smile which transforms
the sad face of the embarrassed sinner.
It is no longer necessary to sail the sea
to admire your infinity
because your infinity dwells within the human heart.

People: We are really happy to be here, Father;
          your Son is in our midst.

What happiness we have here, Father;
your Son is in our midst.
We dream about escaping death
and we go through life without really giving ourselves;
but everything is changed when he is here,
like spring melting
the last traces of ice and snow.
We don't have to fear death
because Jesus has buried for us
the secret of life in death.

People: We are really happy to be here, Father;
          your Son is in our midst.

What happiness we have here, Father;
your Son is in our midst.
We have set the table
with bread and wine;
our love and joy of being together
are shared by all of us;
but everything is changed when he is here,
like a beam of light piercing
the darkness of a cave.
We don't have to make an exact count;
there will be room for everyone;
the bread of our charity will never run out.

People: We are really happy to be here, Father;
          your Son is in our midst.

What happiness we have here, Father;
your Son is in our midst.
And with us are workers and technicians
who transform matter
into a more human usage;
parents and educators who are shaping the freedom
of tomorrow's adults;

doctors and nurses who care for the sick
in order to turn the world into a more fitting
place to live;
motorcycle drivers of every description
who represent to our stilted lives
the exciting pursuit of happiness.
Send your Spirit on us
to transform us with happiness.

People: We are really happy to be here, Father;
         your Son is in our midst.

What happiness we have here, Father;
your Son is in our midst.
His suffering makes our illnesses bearable;
his love renews the love of husbands and wives;
his brotherhood breaks down the divisions
between rich and poor,
between whites and blacks.
It is his glory that we offer to you,
Father,
through him, with him, and in him,
in the unity of the Holy Spirit,
for ever and ever.
Amen.

People: We are really happy to be here, Father;
         your Son is in our midst.

love, death and life

Matthew 17:1-9   *Luke 9:28-36*
Mark 9:2-10   *Philippians 3:17-4:1*

Acclamation/*Transfiguration; Glory.*

Father, you reveal your face
only beyond the desert experience,
only beyond death.

People: Lord, why do you remain so far from us?

Father, you filled your Son, Jesus Christ, with life

at that very moment
when he no longer belonged to himself.

People: The Lord is my light and my salvation.

Christ, you call us each day
to renew our lives
by sharing in your life.

People: I love you, Lord, my rock, my savior.

Christ, you have become the least among us;
you are like broken bread,
passed from hand to hand,
so that we can be alive with your life.

People: Taste and see how good the Lord is.

Spirit, you dwell in us
and you give us strength and courage
in our explorations and hesitations.

People: Lord, let your grace come upon us.

Spirit, inspire enough transforming love in your people
who wish to reshape the whole world.

People: Great glory, eternal praise be yours.

the source

John 2:1-11   *John 19:28-34*
John 4:5-42   *1 Corinthians 10:1-6*
Agape/*Water; Baptism; Progress.*

Father,
we take pride in your presence
for our mastery over nature
and for the creative effectiveness
of our workers and scientists;
For in this awareness you give us
an occasion to encounter you
and a motive to praise you
as we lovingly serve you.

We sing to you
in the murmur of fountains

which make ready their refreshment
for the neighborhoods of our towns.

We sing to you
in the noise of the turbine
which delivers power from water
crashing over the falls.

We sing to you
in the groaning of the ocean
which cultivates in its depths
tomorrow's food.

We sing to you
for water treated by scientists
with a thousand tastes which quench the thirst
and with countless powers to cure us.

* * *

Jesus,
remind us
of what men seek
in pumping water
into their reservoirs and canals,
in unveiling its secrets
and modifying its nature.

Reader: Whoever will drink the water
which I give him
will never thirst again. (John 4:14)

People: My soul thirsts for the living God,
when shall I see him face to face?

* * *

In order to bring this mysterious water
to your brothers
and satisfy those who thirst for
certainty and happiness,
you also experienced thirst for water,
the thirst of a traveler in the midday sun,
the thirst of a man dying on a cross.
In your thirst
you discovered the unfailing source of water
in your Father's love
and this is what you communicate to us

in water changed into wine,
in wine changed into your blood.

Reader: The water which I will give him
           will become in him
           the source of water
           springing out into eternal life. (John 4:14)

People: My soul thirsts for the living God,
           when shall I see him face to face?

*   *   *

May the water poured out in Baptism
not be spilled in vain,
but let that water become
the source of our communion, in faith,
in the mystery of your life.

People: Lord, listen to us;
           Lord, hear us.

May the Church where this living water springs forth
be courageous in revealing to the world
your will for peace and justice
so that all men
might be quenched with your Spirit of love.

People: Lord, listen to us;
           Lord, hear us.

May we not tolerate any longer
vast wastelands
where death and famine hold ruling power,
or concrete cities
with towering monuments
erected by pride and wealth!
Let us be ready to serve all our brothers
with the true results of our efforts.

People: Lord, listen to us;
           Lord, hear us.

Through Christ, your Son, our Lord,
in the unity of the Holy Spirit,
all honor and glory
are yours, Father,
for ever and ever.

People: Amen.

the virtue
of transgression

Matthew 21:12-16
Agape/*Temple; Exclusiveness; Acceptance; Universalism.*

We praise you, God of all men.
You are always uniting all people to yourself.
You chose the Jewish people
to reveal your plan to the Gentiles
by removing barriers and obstacles
which keep nations and cultures apart;
You dwelled in Sion's temple
so that within its walls
would be found
pagans and Jews,
cripples and healthy people,
children and adults
who all share your life;
You wanted your own Son to be born
to realize your plan
which was to have the entire human race
united in an even greater brotherhood.

People: Holy, holy, the Lord is holy.
               His love endures forever.

                                    *   *   *

We call to mind
the work of Jesus among men.
He pardoned sinners
so that they could join the ranks of the just;
he guided cripples
and found them places at the table of healthy people.
he welcomed children
so that they might join with adults
in singing your praise.

People: Hosanna in the highest.
               Blessed is he who comes in the name of the Lord.
               Hosanna in the highest.

To open the temple doors to all men
he transgressed liturgical rules.

He contested
everything in us that stood in the way of universal love.
He who carried in his heart
all of humanity
found himself entirely alone.
Having nothing more to offer except his death,
he willingly gave even that
so all men might be one.

And in order that his intention for unity
might always remain visible,
he likened himself to bread,
made from separate grains,
gathered and baked together;
he took on the wine which we have pressed
from individual grapes.

People: We are mindful
          of your death and resurrection,
          O Christ,
          and we await your return
          while we work with you
          for the union of all men, our brothers.

*   *   *

May we be able, Father,
to purify the Church
of our money changing, our prejudices
and our caste system mentality
which impede the outsider
from finding a home in the Church.
For this is your will.

People: How I rejoiced, when I went out
          to the house of the Lord.

By the action of your Spirit
you are already transforming our hearts;
inspire now in all men
the yearning to live together,
in mutual respect, in sharing and acceptance,
which are the sign of your presence among us.
For this is your will.

People: How I rejoiced, when I went out
          to the house of the Lord.

We want your Church
to be a place of encounter, open to all men;
remove every sentiment of superiority
from your servants and your faithful
so that they may be attentive
to the needs of their brothers;
let your people bring before you
the offering which carries the hopes and expectations
of all men.
For this is your will.

People: How I rejoiced, when I went out
          to the house of the Lord.

You have reunited in the temple
sick people and children,
the poor and the outcast;
inspire in all of your people
an authentic love
so that there will be more warmth for the lonely,
for the despised, a sincere sharing,
for the weak, human support.
For this is the way the new spiritual temple
is constructed
where your Son will be all things to all men
in an eternal act of self giving
for ever and ever.

People: Amen.

wash your eyes
at the fountain

John 9:1-41   *Ephesians 5:8-14*
John 3:14-21

Intercession/*Doctrine; Light; Catechumenate.*

Some people are preparing, throughout this lenten season, to
receive the sacraments of faith. Many Christians whom
selfishness or indifference have blinded try during this same
season to make their life deeper and more real.

Others have confused a particular practice or a particular
thought with the light of Christ and, without knowing it,
become myopic.
For all of them and for all of us, let us unite your petitions.

*   *   *

For all those who are entrusted with teaching within the Church,
may they be aware of how fragile their knowledge is;
may they be open to consult with others
who have experience;
may they be attached to the person of Jesus Christ,
rather than systems of thought;
may they make us more aware of
our need for the ultimate.
Let us pray to the Lord.

People: Be our light, O Christ.

For all who are handicapped at birth,
who are deprived of the normal instruments of communication
and who are too often abandoned as uneducable;
let them pardon the hasty resolve
of those who hope for no new births;
let their life prove
that a man's destiny can never find a full explanation
in a birth defect statistic;
let parents, nurses and doctors
in their response and affection
show faith in the lives and personalities of these children.
Let us pray to the Lord.

People: Be our light, O Christ.

For the people to be baptized,
and for Christians in search of greater light,
that they may persevere in their quest to encounter Jesus Christ;
let them never consider their faith as an acquisition
or a reward for their own efforts,
but rather as a need they have for more light;
may their reborn faith make them realize
their responsibility to share themselves with others.
Let us pray to the Lord.

People: Be our light, O Christ.

difficult children

Luke 15:11-32
Penitential Prayer/*Sin; Conversion; Forgiveness.*

Your younger son, Father,
went his own way.
Didn't he have to leave his Father
to find himself?
But progress in science and technology
win him over with their power and success.
He becomes drunk with his own strength
and tests it at the expense of weaker individuals.
He directs the impersonal forces of automation away from
needs which should be satisfied
and plans not yet realized.
He judges all things by his reason alone
to such a degree
that he no longer recognizes how precious
each gift is
and ignores the love anyone shows him.
People:　Yes, I will get up and go to my Father.

But you offer him your lavishly set banquet table
to make him appreciate the taste of a bread
which is too precious to be sold,
so that he fully discovers the unexpected in your love.
People:　Glory to you for ever and ever.

*　　*　　*

Your prodigal son, Father,
has built his own house.
He uses for materials the money necessary
to possess everything,
including the freedom lost by his brothers.
He promulgates laws and regulations
which he calls justice
to keep all rights in his favor
and to maintain the order
which consecrates his monopolies.
He condemns the innocent and the revolutionary
in the name of his brand of justice;

he violates and kills women and children
in the name of the superiority of his race.

People: Yes, I will get up and go to my Father.

You in turn offer him a generous pardon
to teach him that justice for you
means to give without calculating,
to forgive without measuring,
to justify those who have no right to be justified.

People: Glory to you for ever and ever.

*   *   *

Your prodigal son, Father,
continues his life in us.
He makes his own person
the center of the world.
He has recourse to violence
in order to dominate more effectively
the victims of his universal police force.
He labels his own ideas
absolute truth
and does away with people
who do not think as he does.

People: Yes, I will get up and go to my Father.

And yet you place at his disposition
all that you are
and all that you have,
so that he learns that happiness is
living with others and living for others.

People: Glory to you for ever and ever.

*   *   *

Even his older brother, Father,
revolted against you.
Like us, he does not want to be stripped
of his rights and prerogatives,
to allow anyone else to live beside him.
Like us, he is at this moment
so conscious of his righteousness
and his possession of the truth
that he refuses to encounter his brother;
he is not able to dialogue with the man who is searching.

People: Yes, I will get up and go to my Father.

How amazing it is that you send your first born,
Jesus Christ, our Lord,
to encounter sinners,
to offer your life to people who are searching,
to reveal your love to the weak and poor,
to share bread and wine
with us and with all of mankind.

People: Glory to your for ever and ever.

courage to face life

Ezechiel 37:12-14   *John 11:1-45*
Luke 21:37—22:38   *Philippians 3:8-14*
Eucharist/*Life; Death.*

It is really good to give you thanks,
Father of Jesus Christ;
you accompany us throughout our entire life,
and would this happen if you were going
to abandon us in death?
Despite our original sin,
your presence ennobles our life,
and would this happen
if our life was destined to be dissolved
into nothingness?

We thank you, Father,
for giving us in your risen Son, Jesus Christ,
a meaning to our life
which has worth and yet carries in it
the seeds of death.
That is why we praise your life and glory
as we say:

People: Holy, holy, holy,
the Lord, God of the universe,
heaven and earth are filled with your glory.

In order to share our life
and have us share in yours,

your Son, Jesus Christ,
has come among us.
He lived as all of us live;
he died as all of us die;
but he was convinced
that you would accompany him
into the very jaws of death;
and so he sacrificed his long empty night
to become alive in your glorious daylight.
He has become He Who Lives.

*   *   *

Like bread,
which originates from grain but
must be pulverized before it can nourish us;
like wine,
which comes from crushed grapes
and has to be poured out before we feel its effects;
Jesus lived among us and is now interceding for us with God;
he has been snatched away by death
and in dying he has been reborn.

We offer you, Father of living men,
our human life,
destined for death and yet unique,
temporary and yet precious.
We ask you
to fill each of our days
with an eternity of life
through the body and blood of your Son.

*   *   *

We entrust our dear departed ones
to your memory,
for we know you are faithful
and create anew those whom you love.
We cannot believe they have lived in vain.
We ask you:
let them live long lives in their children and friends,
in the heart of each survivor
who shows his courage to face life.

People: For his great love is without end.

We also entrust to you,
since we share their sorrow,
all those who live in sadness,
experiencing the deep void
of a beloved spouse, a cherished child,
snatched away very quickly by death.
We beg you:
do not let this trial
make sterile their confidence in life.

People: For his great love is without end.

We entrust to you
the victims of violence and war.
Must they believe through our own failings
that evil is stronger than good
and death more powerful than life?
We ask you:
help them keep their hearts open
to love and hope.

People: For his great love is without end.

Finally, we entrust to you
catechumens who are preparing for Baptism,
and Christians who are undergoing a conversion.
Guide them in their quest for the ultimate in life.
We pray:
let them be seized by death
in order to ripen into life,
following the example of your Son.

People: For his great love is without end.

Through him, with him and in him,
all glory be yours, Father,
in the unity of the Holy Spirit,
for life everlasting.

People: Amen.

a man like others

Philippians 2:6-11

Thanksgiving/*Human Life.*

Be praised, Father of Jesus Christ,
for your Son's life
which was like ours in every respect.

He lived our childhood,
a carefree boy,
discovering dependence
by submitting to his parents.

He lived our adolescence,
the awakening of new forces within him;
he gazed freely over the world
and heard so many calls to go beyond himself,
even to the fullest extent of his love.

He worked as a humble carpenter,
placing himself and his time
at the service of others,
convinced of your presence in his activity,
since your way of being with men
consists in serving them.

He took to the spoken word
to defend love and justice;
he became a public man,
vulnerable to the whims of the crowd.
Worshiped or despised,
followed or misunderstood,
he found in your mysterious faithfulness to him
the strength to control these contradictions.

He knew some happy days
and some days that were as somber as night;
he sought the quiet of solitude
to become accustomed to living each day
in communion with you.

He died a premature death,
dramatically holding on to the certainty
that a Father who was always close to him

would not abandon him to annihilation,
but would give him an immortal name.

That is why, on the night he died,
he took bread and wine,
and, while giving thanks to him
whom he constantly relied on for existence,
he made these gifts the promise of resurrection
for himself and his brothers.

That is why we give you thanks, Father,
for the coming of Jesus among us,
for his life offered to each man and to the poorest of men,
for his message of love
which has never stopped resounding in the world:
in the Church and her ministers,
through the sacraments and gifts of the Spirit,
in a living faith and love for all,
by men who make the decision
to make this world a better place.

May every tongue proclaim your name
to bring glory to God our Father!

his body has become accessible

1 Corinthians 11:23-26

Psalm/*Body; Relationship; Communion.*

He handed over his body.
He had already tried to extend his hand,
but no one accepted it.
He had already gazed warmly at the people around him,
but no one looked into his eyes.
He had already walked
the dusty paths of our world,
but how can rocky soil
retain the footprint of a passerby?
The only thing left for him to do

was to give his entire body
so that we might know that he wanted to share everything.

He handed over his body.
He gave the best of himself
and held back nothing of what he had received from men:
a body formed in his mother's womb;
a body nourished by the sweat from his father's brow;
a body touched by the sick,
embraced by the sinful woman,
bruised by rough soldiers.
Wasn't it only fair that he gave us
what made him similar to us?

He handed over his body,
just like a husband offering the best of himself
as he embraces his responsive wife;
like a father sharing bread with his family
as though it were his own flesh;
like a martyr giving himself over to death
so that others might live.
But can a man's body sustain
such intense sharing and love?

That is why the Father gave him
a new body,
responsive to the impulses of the Spirit,
open to limitless encounters with men.

He handed over his body.
And we have become his body:
his hands reaching out to pick up a baby,
his eyes comforting the wayward woman,
his lips smiling to a stranger.
We are so poor in having only a weak body
to express to our brothers the total gift of Jesus;
we are not even successful
in offering a small part of ourselves!

this body being taken down from the cross

Isaiah 52:13—53:12
John 18:1—19:42

Psalm/*Ultimate; Death; Decision.*

Why did he decide to love me
with such an impossible love
that he ripped open his heart?
What did he expect from me?

Why did he decide to offer me
an unreachable star
so that his arms were stretched out and broken on the cross?
What did he expect from me?

Why did he decide to gather
fruit from thorns
so that his own flesh was pierced?
What did he expect from me?

Why did he decide to treat me so gently
as though I am not guilty
of any misdeed?
What did he expect from me?

Why did he gaze at me
with such an intense look
that I cry just thinking about it?
What did he expect from me?

Why did he decide to bring his life into mine
and lead me
where I did not want to go?
What did he expect from me?

bathing in light

Genesis 1:1—2:4
John 8:12

Psalm/*Light; Darkness; Candle.*

The flames cut their way
through the growing obscurity.
Isn't it wonderful that this light,
invented by man,
conquers our fear of darkness
and makes us yearn for a similar light
that pierces and dispels
our interior darkness?

People: The Lord is my light and my salvation.
            Alleluia!

In the obscurity of our doubts
and denials,
the light of the risen Jesus reawakens
our flickering flames.
His new brightness dazzles
the faces of those who have gone before us;
our tired eyes
suddenly discover a new sharpness
and see a world in living color,
with its destiny once hidden from our eyes.

People: The Lord is my light and my salvation.
            Alleluia!

In the obscurity of your mystery,
invisible Father,
we find you.
Some men refuse to acknowledge you
and others acknowledge you only out of habit.
You have pointed out to us the brightness of sunrise
to end our course of blindness.
Our extended hands
grasp your light;
our glances catch each other's eye
and there we find the brightness of the new day
which is dawning upon us.

Our actions take on meaning
under your illumination.
You are our light, Father,
even though by ourselves we are but shadows.

People: The Lord is my light and my salvation.
            Alleluia!

death, we are conducting your funeral

Matthew 28:1-10   *John 20:1-9*
Mark 16:1-7   *Romans 6:3-11*
Luke 24:1-12   *Colossians 3:1-4*
Luke 24:13-35

Eucharist/*Night; Death; Life*
            Recognition; Joy.

It is truly right and just
to give you thanks, Father of Jesus Christ.
This night you raised
your Son
and allowed him to complete
beyond death
the task which he had set out to do
for each of us.
Night of our stubborn refusals
during which your love and Spirit
fill us with boldness and courage.
Night of a weary despair
during which we are faced with injustice and death
and are still awakened by a new drive for liberty.
Night in which you speak to us
in an invisible, almost indiscernible manner
by the mysterious fraternal presence
of your risen Son.

That is why,
united to all those whom death has already led to your life,

and united to those about to come alive through baptism,
we sing the hymn to your glory:

People: Holy, holy, holy Lord,
           God of the universe!
           Heaven and earth are filled with your glory.

*   *   *

You remain with us, Lord Jesus,
and your presence radiates through all the universe.
And yet you choose not to exercise
any unusual power over this world;
you choose not to occupy a privileged place.
You live with men in a simple way,
and the service you offer us is
as ordinary and reserved,
as indispensable and nourishing
as bread and wine.

People: Lord, you are present in the history of men.
           Lord, you are present in this renewed world.

Your glorified body
shows traces of being wounded by men
and your heart, opened by a lance,
has a never ending flow of
blood and water,
Spirit, life and joy.

People: Lord, you are present in the history of men.
           Lord, you are present in this renewed world.

You walk beside us
and your word warms our hearts.
You take your place at our table
and at every table in the world,
set like ours, for your followers,
at this very moment.

*   *   *

Pour out on your Church
your Spirit and light.
May your Church become the place where
all men in their diversity
meet with your Son.

Do not allow your Church to be
an outsider to their lives.
May she discern in each of them
the real presence of your risen Son.

People: Lord, give us a new heart.
            Put in us, Lord, a new spirit.

Share your life and your Spirit with our departed ones.
It is our fate to die,
and they have died
either because others have snatched away their lives
or because they died,
giving their last drop of blood
so that their brothers and children might live.
In each of them, Father,
it is your breath of life
which came and went.

People: Lord, give us a new heart.
            Put in us, Lord, a new spirit.

Pour out your Spirit and joy
on new Christians
who find deeper meaning in their lives
by asking to be baptized.
With the rest of the Church,
help them to recognize you
in their faithfulness to Christ,
and see that they partake in the Church's happiness.

People: Lord, give us a new heart.
            Put in us, Lord, a new spirit.

*   *   *

Jesus Christ, you are involved
in what happens to us;
you are our blood brother, and yet you are called "Lord";
you who tasted of our earthly condition
are now raised to God's life;
do not be distant from us,
inaccessible and hidden.
Teach us to pray:

People: Our Father, Who are in heaven. . . . .

on the belief of the apostles

Luke 24:13-35
John 20:1-9

Profession of Faith

Do you believe in one God, the Father,
whose Son lived among us,
whose Word sustains our life and renews it
for he is Life?

People: We do believe.

Do you believe in his Son, Jesus Christ,
born among us and risen,
whose decision to free his brothers,
by loving them at the price of his own death,
has transformed our human condition?

People: We do believe.

Do you believe in their Spirit
who lives among us.
He made the apostles' faith come alive
and makes our brotherhood real.
He is present in the Gospel word,
in sacramental actions,
and in the commitment of Christians.
He has begun to transform the world
into God's kingdom.
He gives us hope
in our own resurrection.

People: We do believe.

trying to catch sight of him

John 20:19-29   *Acts 2:42-47*
                         1 John 5:1-6

Agape/*Faith; Weakness; Love.*

Be praised, Father.
From you Jesus took on life again,
for you did not wish to have
the one you loved during his whole life
actually to lose your love
as he lost his life for us.
You fashioned him a new body
so that his friendship would embrace every man.
He is present to each of us,
incognito, almost undetectible.
He is the secret kept from everyone,
anonymous, like a stranger on the road.

We would like to touch him,
with more than the tips of our fingers,
and follow him,
but his glory blinds our eyes;
he is always, it seems, just around the corner.
We would like to see him, hear him,
but our ears are closed to the truth.
We wish to recognize him
but our thoughts stiffle his.
We want to speak to him
but our words interrupt his.
We want to be able to love him,
if our hearts had but a spark of love,
to live with him,
worn out and sad as we are.

But we believe in your word
and in your word
we entrust our existence
as you tell us that the Spirit lives in us,
and we are born once again.
We believe that our light, ordinary words

carry the weight of eternity.
Let our earthly tasks build your kingdom;
let our faithfulness to each other
be a true echo of your love.

We believe that your Spirit
can give to our table the dimensions of the world
because on our table we display
the same bread and the same wine
which Jesus made the memorial
of his universal brotherhood.

May our hearts keep this table open,
with all those who,
scattered over the whole world,
wish to see further than their eyes permit,
and choose to love even
when there's a danger of losing their lives;
with all those who in the Church
urge us to put aside pettiness
and witness for us the faith of the apostles;
with all those who suffer in their flesh
and discover, little by little,
the full love which a worn out body can give;
with all those who question
the absence of a loved one;
with all those who have entered into death,
open to your love,
yearning for your life.

Father, receive our Amen;
it is electrified by the indistinguishable murmurs
of all people, our brothers and sisters,
and by the shout of your Son, Jesus Christ.
Through him, with him and in him,
are to you, Father, and to you, Holy Spirit,
all honor and all glory,
forever and ever.

People: Amen.

recognition

Luke 24:13-35

Agape/*Awareness; Presence of God.*

We recognize you, Father,
in Jesus Christ, our brother,
your Word and your Expression;
in the scope of his glance
which dissipates evil;
in the direct tone of his voice
which sets our hearts on fire;
in the silence
which dignifies death.
We recognize you
like a child who has never seen his father
and yet picks him out in a crowd
because the same blood flows through their veins.

We recognize you, Father,
thanks to Jesus Christ, our brother,
your Word and your Expression;
in that love in our hearts
which carries us further than we dare to go;
in that service toward our brothers
which makes us like your Son.
We recognize you
like a man recognizes an old friend
as though they had never been separated.

We ask you to recognize your children
in the huge throng of people on earth;
they have searched for happiness all day long
and dusk is now closing in
and they have not yet found that happiness.

We ask you to recognize your children
among those people throughout the world
who like us are gathered
around the same bread and the same cup
to praise your name.

We ask you to recognize your children
among the people who speak to us about you

and strengthen our hesitating faith;
among those who speak to us about our brothers
and revive our dormant charity.

We ask you to recognize your children
in those whom death has distorted
who are restored when you gaze lovingly upon them;
in those who try to separate themselves from you,
but whom your love reconciles to you.

And hasten the day, Father,
when we will see you face to face,
when no one need tell us
who you are,
for our hearts will be overflowing with your life
and never feel empty again!

forgiveness for sins

Luke 24:35-48   *1 John 2:1-5*
Acts 3:13-19

Penitential Prayer/*Sin; Conversion; Forgiveness.*

We give you thanks, Father,
because your Son has accepted
an unheard of death between robbers,
because you have accepted your Son
in that repulsive condition.

We recall the thanksgiving of Jesus
who, on the night before he died,
prayed over the bread and the cup,
with gladness in his heart,
because he knew you accepted him.

Also accept us
because we have an advocate
to plead our cause with you;
since his death did not frighten away your love,
do not let our sins scare away your forgiveness!

We know that you accept us
in whatever condition we find ourselves,
and for this we give you thanks,
with peace in our hearts as we realize
that a gesture on your part
restores us to what we should be.

Send forth your Spirit into our hearts;
may he teach us to accept ourselves
without covering up our misery;
may he help us to renounce
our hurried, so-called acceptable methods
in our own attempts to erase our shortcomings;
may he help us to see ourselves
in the way that you look at us.

a shepherd who is always searching

John 10:11-18

Acclamation/*Spirit; Shepherd; Life.*   .

We praise you, our living God.
In your repose
our fatigue finds its resting place;
in your healing
our sicknesses are cured.
in your life
even our death is transfigured;
in your love
our hatred disappears.

People: To you, O God, let praise come from all people,
             let all people praise you with one voice.

We praise you, God, source of life.
You have worked wonders in your son, Jesus Christ.
You cured him from the ailments
which he contracted on our behalf;
you acknowledged him
when we refused to believe in him;
you stayed at his side
in his struggle to win against great odds;
you raised him from the death
which destroyed the power of death over our lives.

People: To you, O God, let praise come from all people,
             let all people praise you with one voice.

We praise you, Father of life.
You send the Spirit on us
to fashion us into your children.
The Spirit inspires those who speak about you,
he accompanies freedom songs,
he travels the roads which bring people together;
he never forgets those who lose their way
as they struggle for a more just world;
he watches over the person who goes astray
and gives new life to anyone who gives up his own life.

People: To you, O God, let praise come from all people,
         let all people praise you with one voice.

a road...a house

John 14:1-10

Agape Prayer/*Road; House; Welcome.*

We give you thanks, Father,
because you open for us the door of your home
where you unveil secrets for us.
We praise you
because to get there you point out to us
the right road,
Jesus, your dear Son,
who came to tell us about you.
That is why with all the living,
together with those
who are already reunited in your house,
we pay homage to your name:

People: Holy, holy, the Lord is holy;
         his love endures forever.

                    *   *   *

We praise you, Jesus Christ,
for showing us the road
which leads to your house.
You have payed with your life
for your concern to remove
all blockades and obstacles
which lie in our path.
It was in this way, as you know,
that others have died
who wanted to give more freedom to their brothers!

You have done everything
to have us gain entrance to your home.
How moving it is, as you know,
to welcome those whom you love!
The young lady who introduces her fiance

to her parents for the very first time;
old friends who meet again by accident
who are "wined and dined" at home
because it's at home
where the best of ourselves can always be expressed.

This bread on the table for each of us
and this cup of wine tipped to our lips,
the joy of finding ourselves here together,
ready to open ourselves
to what may be new and unknown;
in that spirit
we offer these gifts to you, Lord.
They are the remembrance of what
you have done for us,
on the night before you died.
They are the promise of what you reserve for us,
where you live, close to the Father.

*   *   *

Be present, Lord Jesus,
to your Church.
May she express
concern for the progress of people.
May she forego presenting herself
as the house of God
and accept the task of being
the humble road to that house.

People: Hear us, Lord of glory!

Pray to your Father for each baptized person.
Let us all share in the task of renewing our world
and in the initiatives which make it
a more just and more fitting place to live.

People: Hear us, Lord of glory!

Beg your Father to send his Spirit.
Let him give to this world where we live
a new complexion,
enlightened by peace, glowing with love.

People: Hear us, Lord of glory!

Beg your Father to welcome into his house,
where the secret of his life is unveiled,

those among us who have departed.
May he especially recognize
those who die
in a death similar to your own,
freely offered
so that all men might live in freedom.

People: Hear us, Lord of glory!

Pray also to the Father for those houses
where the shades have been pulled down to hide
death and despair,
hatred and loneliness.
Do not allow those who live there
to turn into hell
what is actually a foretaste of your home.

People: Hear us, Lord of glory!

And Father, let your name be known by men
through him, with him, and in him,
now and for ever,
world without end.

People: Amen!

where does this road lead?

John 14:1-10
Psalm/*Road; Truth; Life; House.*

Are you really that road which,
like a steamroller, runs over our life,
heading toward who knows where?

Are you really that life
which unfolds before us as we hope
for a few breaks in life?   *more clarity*

Are you really that truth
which takes hold of us
less strongly than our fears and doubts?

Are you that house
which no longer warms our hearts
which are frozen over with bitterness?

*   *   *

Are you that road
leading to nowhere
because it runs beyond the visible?

Are you that life
which is given only to end in death
since life itself is meant to be given away?

Are you that truth
to which we sacrifice ourselves
when everything seems to collapse around us?

Are you that house
without walls, having no roof, no locks,
which is actually called friendship?

*   *   *

If you are all these, Jesus,
then I believe in you.
All of this is so human
that only God could have thought it up.

no longer will there be a temple

Revelation 21:15-22

Psalm/*Temple; Institution; Religion; Spirit.*

No more temple will we see;
Jesus Christ who is the fullness of all things
will be close to each of us,
present in everything.

Help us, Lord, to be quick in destroying
the temples of our good consciences
where we dispense ourselves from reaching out to men;
the temples of our idolatries
where we make wholehearted sacrifices
to the gods of power and hatred.

Send forth your Spirit:
our prayer desperately needs
his love and his truth

to put together at least the beginning
of a prayer of eternal praise.

People: I rejoiced, alleluia,
when I set out
toward the house of the Lord.

*   *   *

No more priests will we find.
Jesus Christ himself will lead the way
into God's presence
for all the people he has saved.

Help, Lord, the ministers torn apart
by doubt and fear
to recognize in a clear way
that their service has only one purpose:
to teach your people
the harmonies of your praise.

Send forth your Spirit:
our activity really needs
his brotherhood
so that everyone in the world
might start to gather
in the dwelling place
which he prepares for us.

People: I rejoiced, alleluia,
when I set out
toward the house of the Lord.

*   *   *

No more structures will remain.
The Church will be dissolved into the Kingdom
where each man will reign forever.

Help us, Lord, to reevaluate
habits and challenges,
old styles and new methods.

Send forth your Spirit:
our language so keenly needs
his truth
to resist the glitter of new phrases
and to discover the true enchantment
of the living name of our God.

People: I rejoiced, alleluia,
            when I set out
            toward the house of the Lord.

* * *

There will be no more laws.
For God's Word will enlighten
the mind of each man
and stir him to respond.

Help us, Lord, to make ready this city
in our awareness of the need others have for us,
and in the decisions we make
to be of greater service to them.

Send forth your Spirit:
our world cries out in the need
to admit its failure to love
so that everything which is the Father's
may one day be the possession
of each of our brothers.

People: I rejoiced, alleluia,
            when I set out
            toward the house of the Lord.

he will throw open
god's kingdom to us

Acts 1:1-11   *Matthew 28:16-20*
Luke 24:44-53   *Mark 16:15-20*

Intercession/*Name; Power; Life; Universe.*

God, you have given your own name
to Jesus, our brother.
We are grateful to you for inviting us,
each and every day, despite our weakness,
to be joined to him.
And just as he is constantly presenting to you
all those whom he has known here below,
accept our own concern

for those whom we meet each day:
our husband, our wife,
our parents, our children
and those who confide in us,
our friends and adversaries,
our cooks and our fellow workers,
and all those who remain nameless
while they share with us the same life
and the same worries.

People: Lord, give glory not to us
               but to your name.

God, you have given your own strength
to Jesus, our brother.
Death had transfigured him
but you received him into your life
and kept him present
among us.
Consecrate us too in the service of our brothers
as we think of others first.
Let your strength make us
attentive and sensitive
toward those who suffer and are forgotten.
Let your strength bend our selfishness
into respect and tolerance.

People: Lord, give glory not to us
               but to your name.

God, you gave the immensity of space
to Jesus, our brother.

No other empire
will ever dominate man again.
Let our activity in the world
enrich his reign with the secrets of each culture
and the discoveries of each nation.
May our hearts be open
to love everyone
and support everyone.
May we find the words to dialogue
with every misery and every joy
and live fully the winters and summers of time.

Let our desires be detached from mirages
and be focused on the real tasks
which you gave us to accomplish.

People: Lord, give glory not to us
but to your name.

God, you have given the fullness of your life
to Jesus, our brother.
He enjoys your intimacy
and your love goes through him
to reach us and our brothers.
May our everyday efforts
radiate with the certainty
that we live with you.
May our love be transfigured
by the warmth of your life.
Father, make our faith grow,
because it is difficult for us to rely
on your intangible presence
and to satisfy ourselves
with your very discrete way of serving our needs,
because we set such high standards
in terms of measuring output and efficiency.

People: Lord, give glory not to us
but to your name.

that word which i was waiting to hear from you

Acts 2:1-11

Thanksgiving/*Word; Silence.*

Be praised
by the words given to man
to dialogue and open up,
to question and respond,
for saying, "I love you"
and for praying "Our Father."

People: The Spirit of the Lord fills
the universe, alleluia!
He knows every word, alleluia!

Be praised
by the words given to man
in which scholars and thinkers
unveil to their brothers
new and better ways;
in which poems and songs
discover in each situation
the joy of being full of life and wonderment.

People: The Spirit of the Lord fills
the universe, alleluia!
He knows every word, alleluia!

Be praised
by the silence offered to man
to comprehend the echo
of words which he cherishes;
to take the time
to control his lips;
to pronounce difficult and simple words
which begin to describe your mystery.

People: The Spirit of the Lord fills
the universe, alleluia!
He knows every word, alleluia!

Be praised
by the words given to man
so that he communicates to his brothers
his ideals and his belief,
the hope for your kingdom
and the good news of your love,
that word-made-flesh
in Jesus Christ, our Lord,
in whom everything finds its meaning
and tells us who you are.

People: The Spirit of the Lord fills
the universe, alleluia!
He knows every word, alleluia!

Be praised
by the words given to man
which you need not repeat:
The Word, firm as the bread we are eating,
intoxicating as the first sip of wine in the morning;
This Word sounds stronger than our doubts,
erases our infidelities,
steadies our shaky knees,
and makes our eyes dance with enthusiasm.

People: The Spirit of the Lord fills
the universe, alleluia!
He knows every word, alleluia!

climbing out of the river

Matthew 3:13-17   *Luke 3:15-22*
Mark 1:9-13

Eucharist/*Baptism; Freedom;*
       Beloved Son; Unity.

Be praised, Father,
for your Son, Jesus Christ.
He came to the Jordan
to join up with the small remnant of Yahweh's Poor
and to share in their hope for your kingdom.
In order to merit his title as "Beloved Son,"
he wanted to reassemble all men,
warring classes, separated tribes;
he tried to enlighten his brothers
and placed himself at their service
so that they could one day be freed from evil;
he established his lordship over all things
and, in order to conquer death,
he delivered himself over to the unknown.

*   *   *

To make certain that death might never have the last word,
and freedom might never be choked off,
and the one same table might unite
all the sons of the kingdom,
and, Father, so that your will might be accomplished,
Jesus took bread and wine
and offered them to us
as the measure of his love;
And we repeat this action of the Lord
in the grace of his Spirit
and in praise of his Name.

*   *   *

Reunited around this welcoming table,
we receive from you, Father, with full awareness,
our mission of being on earth
attentive to liberate men
from the ensnarements invented by the powerful,

68

from the obstacles to our freedom
which are built up by fear and pride.

Gathered in this friendly home
and being aware of each other,
we share this bread and drink from this cup.

You are challenging us
to be, in your Son,
the stewarts of unity and exchange,
by being sensitive to the means placed at our disposal
through progress and science
to bring better communication between men
and in so doing make them come alive with your life.

Accept, Father, our good will
as you accepted the offering of your Son on the Cross.
Let our resolution become efficacious and constructive,
outgoing and selfless;
let our resolution be born again
in the heart of each baptized person
so that in being a sign of your love
each person earns for himself
the title of beloved son.
Let our resolution be born again
in the heart of every bishop and priest
so that they might be the object of your love
in Jesus Christ, your Son, our Lord.

People:　Through him, with him and in him,
　　　　　all honor and glory are yours, Father,
　　　　　in the unity of the Holy Spirit,
　　　　　for ever and ever. Amen.

prayer to the dove

Matthew 3:13-17　　　*Luke 3:15-22*
Mark 1:9-13
Psalm/*Baptism; Investiture.*

Clear away, O God, those heavy clouds
which gather before us
and close our eyes to reality.

People: For you alone, Lord, are our Father.
Make your voice heard once again
and speak into our stuffed ears
so that we may be servants and beloved sons.
People: For you alone, Lord, are our Father.
Urge our clenched fists
to reach out
to pull our hopeless brothers
out of the waters of hatred and misery.
People: For you alone, Lord, are our Father.
Send forth your Spirit to inspire us
so that our works and our thoughts
become signs of your love before men,
signs of their hope of meeting you face to face.
People: For you alone, Lord, are our Father.
Be here with us in these places which lack love,
where people are bleeding,
where they slave and die in silence.
You know now what makes our lives
like an endless night.
People: For you alone, Lord, are our Father.

you have seized me, lord.

1 Samuel 3:3-10   *John 1:29-34*
                       John 1:35-42

Intercession/*Vocation.*

For the family surroundings
which have stirred up
our yearning to serve,
our vocation and our belief,
be praised, Lord.
For the friend we meet on the street
whose genuine enthusiasm and witness
recreate commitment and faithfulness
in us once again,
be praised, Lord.

For the situations and trials
which are part of each day
and which speak to us of you,
be praised, Lord.

* * *

Here we are in your presence, Father,
we who have freely chosen
our task, our state in life and our commitment.
Let us live out our calling in a more fruitful way
in accepting our limitations;
let us become more disposed
to serve those who are around us.
And you, Father, may your concern for us
encourage us
and continue to give us support.

* * *

Here we are in your presence, Father,
we who believe we have been tricked
in the choice of our state in life.
Failure has extinguished our love,
and discouragement sterilizes our actions.
May our brothers support us
and may they accept our discouragement.
And you, Father, may your warm concern for us
help us to love ourselves once again.

* * *

Here we are in your presence, Father,
we who have chosen our vocation
with limited freedom and scope of vision.
May our poverty
authorize us to call out to our brothers
whose life seems fuller than ours.
May their way of life serve
to help us be freer in choosing our vocation.

you call out and
the deaf begin to hear

Nahum 8:1-10
Matthew 4:12-17
Mark 1:14-20

Luke 4:14-21
1 Corinthians 1:10-17
1 Corinthians 12:26-30

Agape/*Word*

It is good, Lord, that all of us together
give glory to you;
you are the Father of men
and they become your heaven and earth.
Through the word which they have received from you,
they name all things,
enter into relationships with their fellow man,
sing about happy and sad situations in life
and are joined together in a common purpose.
We thank you for these words
which we share among us
to carry us on to greater courage, love and discovery.

You are dwelling in inaccessible light,
and no human word can fully name you!
But you decided to speak to man
and dwell within his innermost being,
within the saints and the poor,
within prophets and sinners.

People: The Lord is with us, Alleluia.
He protects us every day of our lives. Alleluia.
His word resounds. Alleluia.
His word is truth. Alleluia.

* * *

You are present by your Spirit
in every action of our lives,
from the Exodus out of Egypt
to modern scientific discoveries,
from the return from Exile
to the liberations which take place today.
In the hour you selected,
you spoke to us with power

in the person of your Son.
In his sacrifice on the cross
we find your decision
to overcome sin and death;
in his life and resurrection
we find your decision
to bring together the whole universe in him.
That is why, reunited around this table,
we are mindful of the night
when he was handed over.

People: We live by his Word. Alleluia.
Each day of our life. Alleluia.
Hearing and receiving. Alleluia.
The word of the Lord. Alleluia.

* * *

Most kind Father,
do not abandon us;
let the Spirit of Jesus live among us!
Let him open our eyes
to the works of your Word;
let him unloose our tongue
and we will proclaim with courage
humanity transfigured in Christ
through the witness of our lives.
Let him animate the servants of the Word
as he inspired the prophets
and messengers of the Good News.
Let him attract all men
with full respect to their freedom
so that they might become attached to your word.
For it is in your word, become flesh in Jesus Christ.

People: That all honor and all glory. Alleluia.
Are given to you, God our Father. Alleluia.
Now and for ever. Alleluia.
As it has been from the beginning. Alleluia.

utopia of happiness

Matthew 5:1-12
1 Corinthians 1:26-31

Eucharist/*Poverty; Wisdom; Foolishness;*
Utopia; Holiness.

We praise you, Father,
for your loving decision
to communicate your holiness and wisdom
in the heart of every man,
and in the material things which man transforms.
You are truly holy, Father,
and our joy overflows as we say to the world:

People: Holy, holy, holy Lord,
God of the Universe,
heaven and earth are filled with your glory.
Hosanna in the highest.
Blessed is he who comes in the name of the Lord.
Hosanna in the highest.

*   *   *

Blessed is he who has come
to share his holiness with us.
He lives among us
sharing in our poverty
and dreams of glory and happiness.
He becomes united to the men crushed by the powerful
and gives meaning to their oppression.
He shares in the humility
and nonviolence of pacifists
and recognizes in them the reflection of your love.
He partakes of the hunger and thirst
of poor people and sinners
and turns all that suffering into a promise
of life and happiness.
He communicates in the foolishness of men
to describe the utopia of your wisdom.
And in order to fix his attitude,
once and for all,
on the night of his Passion,

he shared a meal with poor, restless men,
and gave to that meal a new meaning,
the meaning of love and sharing,
death accepted and destroyed.

People: Remember Jesus Christ,
risen from the dead.
If we die with him,
with him we will live.
If we suffer with him,
with him we will reign.
In him is our glory,
in him our salvation.

*   *   *

Send on us
your Spirit of holiness.
Let him teach us how to recognize
in the hunger of the poor
the sharing of bread,
in their desire for instruction
their very slow efforts
toward cultural assimilation,
in the desire for freedom
the revolt against oppression,
in the meekness of pacifists
the violence of the oppressed.
Here are some of the baffling signs
of the utopia of holiness
actually alive in the heart of every man.

People: O Lord, hear us and have mercy.

May we be able to be attentive to your Spirit of holiness.
For our efforts for peace and sharing,
our pacifist movements and our revolutions,
are too uncertain and equivocal
to merit by themselves to be acknowledged
as signs of your love.
Help us
to strip ourselves of all selfishness
and to extend our hand to others
without worrying about our self interests.

People: O Lord, hear us and have mercy.

Help us to be attentive
to your Spirit of holiness.
Help us guide those who exercise power
so that they will respect the dignity of men
and provide in the lives of the most unhappy of men
an openness to your love.

People: O Lord, hear us and have mercy.

Help us to be open
to your Spirit of holiness
so that we may join
in the witness of our forefathers in the faith
and communicate with them
in the life of your Son, Jesus Christ.

People: O Lord, hear us and have mercy.

Through him, with him and in him,
all honor and glory
are yours, God our Father,
in the unity of the Spirit.

People: Amen.

we who have not seen god

Isaiah 6:1-8   *John 20:19-29*
Luke 5:1-11   *1 Corinthians 5:1-11*

Agape/*Faith; Vision; Earthly Condition.*

Isaiah saw your glory, Father,
before telling the whole world about it.
He understood your holiness from close up
before demanding that holiness from his people.
He was caught up with your honor
before reforming the political situation.
He had his lips scorched
to sing with dignity
the hymn to your glory:

People: Holy, holy, holy Lord, God of the Universe.
Heaven and earth are filled with your glory.
Hosanna in the highest.

Blessed is he who comes in the name of the Lord.
Hosanna in the highest.

But no angel comes upon us
to purify our lips.
Heaven and earth are now filled
with the glory of men.
Perhaps we would be
devout apostles of your holiness
if we had seen your powerful throne
and the cherubim who serve you.

* * *

The disciples contemplated your might
as your Son performed
the abundant catch of fish in their nets.
They immediately left their family
to follow Jesus as they trusted
that they would become
the joyfilled fishers of men!

People: Now that we have recognized your grace
in choosing us,
we have responded in joy to your call.

We are also fishers of men
and several of us have left our nets.
But we have never seen any miraculous catch!
We would rather have Jesus toil with us
all night long and not catch anything.

* * *

The apostles saw the risen Christ;
he appeared to them and ate with them;
he explained everything to them
by using the scriptures.
And they believed with enthusiasm
as the entire world resounded with their word:

People: The Lord is risen, Alleluia.
Like springtime, a new day dawns on us,
like springtime, Christ has returned.

We are today's witnesses of a resurrection
which we have not seen;

come now Lord;
show your glory and we will believe in you.

* * *

But your glory, Father,
is the heart of man,
and your holiness
the love which you witness to us.
Your greatness in that you keep nothing to yourself,
your honor in that you are very close to us.
We give you thanks
for the manifestation among us of your majesty
in Jesus of Nazareth, whom you chose
from among men
to be the glory of your poverty.
He lived as all people live
in joy and sadness,
in fleeting pleasure,
in love which sometimes lasts for a few moments longer.
He knew quick success
and the loneliness of a prophet
abandoned as though he had a contagious disease.
His actions were often misunderstood,
and his words subject to various interpretations.
Through all these hardships,
he went his own way
—which is also your way, Father—
and on the last night of his life
spent with his close friends,
he became like
bread broken for sharing,
wine poured out in pursuit of friendship.

People: We proclaim your death, Lord,
            we celebrate your resurrection,
            we await your coming in glory.

In Jesus who was faithful to his human life
even to death, death on a cross,
we acknowledge your glory, Father,
and that's why we believe
that you have raised him up.

* * *

Let your Spirit come
to teach us how to live
our everyday life and its problems
in the intimacy of your presence and holiness.

Let your Spirit come
to teach us to live your life
where we have already settled for
living only our own life and death.

Let your Spirit come
to purify our lips in secret
so that we will be bold enough
to say your name among the words we use
to describe our loves and our struggles.

Then indeed
we will have seen your glory
which you manifest only in your Son,
in the unity of the Holy Spirit
for ever and ever.

People: Amen.

your judgment is clearly spoken

Luke 6:20-26   *1 Corinthians 15:12-20*
Matthew 5:1-11

Psalm/*Poverty; Hunger; Sadness;
        Oppression; Intelligence; Death.*

1. We give you thanks, Lord,
   without really knowing why.

   You promised riches to the poor
   and misery never ceases to grow in the world;
   You promised happiness to the dispossessed,
   but their wealthy brothers share with them
   only a small part of their riches.

They build their own comfort
with a profit made from unscrupulous exploitations.

But we thank you
for you shared the weakness of the poor
and through their eyes scanned
the wide horizon of hopelessness.

People: Rise up, Lord, do not forget us!

* * *

2. We give you thanks, Lord,
   without really knowing why.

   You promised the hungry
   enough bread to fill them,
   and hunger reigns over much of the world;
   you promised them happiness
   but their overweight brothers
   send them care packages
   only when it's convenient.
   The affluent arm the poor for war
   but refuse them the real means
   for self development.

   But we thank you
   for sharing your bread
   with those who are hungry
   and with those who are filled
   in order to give rise in all of them
   of that hunger for love and justice
   which made you die on the cross.

   People: Rise up, Lord, do not forget us.

* * *

3. We give you thanks, Lord,
   without really knowing why.

   You promised consolation and laughter
   to those who weep,
   but their comfortable brothers
   refuse the lonely old man
   the company which would be like heaven for him.
   People are complaining about the scandal,
   but are not willing to understand

the despair of young people on drugs.
Confronted with suffering and sadness,
they observe the prudent silence
kept by those who choose to look the other way.

But we thank you
because you cried too
and accepted the sorrow-laden privilege
of carrying the lamentations of the entire world
before your Father.

People: Rise up, Lord, do not forget us.

* * *

4. We give you thanks, Father,
   without really knowing why.

   You promised peace to the oppressed
   but persecution and war
   have destroyed so many lives;
   you promised them happiness
   but their powerful brothers
   kill them with napalm or put them in prison;
   their power is transformed
   into violent police action.
   Hands made to build and embrace
   are actually choking and killing.

   But we thank you
   for deciding to undergo
   repression on the cross,
   certain that your unfailing love
   would, each day, transform
   a little more of the world.

   People: Rise up, Lord, do not forget us.

* * *

5. We give you thanks, Father,
   without really knowing why.

   You promised to guileless people
   a wisdom which could be compared to yours;
   you promised them happiness,
   but their intellectual brothers,
   drunk with science and technology,

allow people to be locked into
a soft, easy life.
Progress stultifies us;
comfort makes us compromise ourselves;
affluence weakens us.

But we thank you
for thinking like us,
by growing in wisdom and intelligence
in order to reveal to us
the secret of your Father's way of thinking.

People: Rise up, Lord, do not forget us.

*   *   *

6. We give you thanks, Father,
without really knowing why.

You brought back to life
the dead carried in on stretchers to you;
you promised them happiness,
but their lives remain commonplace,
like crabgrass and weeds
which are born haphazardly into life
and are destined for oblivion.

But we thank you
for sharing our death;
you taught us how life is to be lived for death,
and how we die
so that we may live and help others come alive.

the house with the shades pulled down

Leviticus 19:1-2, 17-18   *Matthew 5:38-48*
1 Samuel 26:7-9, 22-24   *Luke 6:27-38*

Intercession/*Love; Charity;*
                    Turning Back; Opposition.

Brothers,
so many men and women

waste away and get shriveled up
in a universe reduced to fit their scope of vision,
Let us ask the Spirit of the Lord
to open up their hearts
to a greater and stronger love.

People: Lord, source of love,
          make us burn with charity.

For families turned in on themselves,
exclusive in their affections,
indifferent to the external world;
so that they may notice
the needs and joys which surround them,
let us pray to the Lord!

People: Lord, source of love,
          make us burn with charity.

For sad and isolated towns
divided by clannish quarrels;
for troubled towns
where teens rebel
and no longer hope in adults;
for slum neighborhoods
where, with no assistance from the rest of society,
the poor and alienated are dying,
let us pray to the Lord!

People: Lord, source of love,
          make us burn with charity.

For groups, classes, antagonistic races,
which see their own vengeance and their own security
in absolute, unbending terms;
for politicians
and national and international diplomats
so that their concern for the common good
goes beyond their defense
of the narrow interests of the constituents,
let us pray to the Lord!

People: Lord, source of love,
          make us burn with charity.

For Christian communities
entrenched in their dogmas and practices,

that they may guard against seeing an enemy
in someone who disagrees,
a sinner in the unbeliever;
for the most uncompromising among us
in whose eyes every dialogue is already a compromise
and adaptation to another's viewpoint means
abandoning the truth,
let us pray to the Lord.

People: Lord, source of love,
make us burn with charity.

For all of us gathered in the Eucharist,
so that throughout the entire world
those who today partake of the same bread
and the same communion cup
may become witnesses of the Lord
who made himself all things for all men;
so that each of us willingly gives our life and time
for the happiness of others,
let us pray to the Lord.

People: Lord, source of love,
make us burn with charity.

to make the world
an appealing place to live

Matthew 5:38-48   *Luke 6:27-38*
Matthew 22:34-40   *John 13:31-35*

Eucharist/*Love*

It is good that all of us assembled here
give thanks to you,
Father of Jesus,
for you understand what our human life is all about.
Because you are good,
you made us for one another.
The love between husband and wife
is part of your secret of love,
and so is the tenderness of a mother and father,

the manner in which children need to be held,
and the desire each man has to be close to his brother.

We thank you
for all those who help and console us,
for those who give us guidance and grant us pardon,
for those who keep us company
in our hours of distress and loneliness.
We thank you
for all we can accomplish
through our work
for the well being of others.

God of men,
we praise you
for the most well rounded man,
Jesus Christ, your Son.
He showed us how to live and how to die.
He taught us the true meaning of
generosity, faithfulness,
courage, obedience and love.

Together with his Church throughout the entire world,
we add our weak voices
as we sing . . .

People: Holy, holy, the Lord is holy.
            His great love is without end.

*   *   *

Father,
you dwell beyond the far reaches of light
and no one has ever seen you;
still we believe you are the God of men.
You live among us,
you are near to us,
like the closeness enjoyed by intimate friends.

So you appeared
in Jesus, your Son.
He told us that you are our Father:
that you are goodness and generosity,
that you are the fullness of love.
We have assembled around this table
as children of one large family.

On his last night, when he was given over,
when his hour had come,
he gave his friends the sign of his far reaching love.

People: Jesus died, faithful to his mission,
and full of love for people.
He will live forever,
the First Born of all those who decide to love.

*   *   *

May your Spirit place us around this table
with all those who make the decision
to witness love in the world.
In union with the bishop of Rome
who is the loving servant of local churches;
in union with people who consecrate their life
to bring about peace and mutual forgiveness among nations;
in union with those who labor
to persuade rich nations
to give foreign aid with no strings attached;
in union with the men and women
who generously share
their abundance and their substance
so that our hard world
becomes a more worthy dwelling place
where Jesus Christ fulfills the desires in each man's heart.

People: Through him, with him and in him,
all honor and glory
are yours, God our Father,
in the unity of the Holy Spirit,
for ever and ever.
Amen.

do not fear, little flock

Romans 8:14-17
Penitential Prayer/*Father; Panic;
Fear; Trust.*

Lord, we are frightened by your justice
measured according to our standards:

an eye for an eye, a tooth for a tooth.
And we are uneasy as we consider
our good actions and our bad actions.
You want us to call you Father,
yet how can your children live in this slavish mentality,
having no trust in your love
which pardons and justifies?

People: The Lord is my light and my salvation,
              whom shall I fear?

We are frightened by each other.
Our nation is mobilizing out of fear of border invasions;
management dreads union workers;
blacks live terrorized by whites;
panic leads to violence and hatred.
You want us to call you Father,
yet how can your children be constantly killing one another,
and not be discovering their brotherhood
and common heritage
which can be found in your love and your life?

People: The Lord is my light and my salvation,
              whom shall I fear?

We are frightened of our liberty,
created so that we might discover life.
We dread risk and adventure
which call us to go beyond ourselves.
Rigid ready-made formulas
dispense us from thinking and becoming committed.
You want us to call you Father,
yet how can your children give up so easily
in our work of renewing hearts,
a work made possible by your love?

People: The Lord is my light and my salvation,
              whom shall I fear?

We are frightened by reforms and changes
which force us to question how we perceive ourselves.
Old people fly off the handle
when confronted by the young;
those in authority barricade themselves
to solidify their positions.

You want us to call you Father,
yet how can your children be so opposed to each other,
failing to share in the same riches
which overflow so abundantly in your house?
People: The Lord is my light and my salvation,
                whom shall I fear?

for a new meal

Exodus 24:3-8   *Mark 14:12-26*
1 Corinthians 10:16-17   *Luke 9:11-17*
1 Corinthians 11:23-29   *John 6:51-59*
Agape/*Meal.*

We praise you, Father of Jesus Christ.
You keep close to us
so that through our labor and toil
we might give each day's bread
to our families and our brothers who are starving.
You put in our hearts
the joy of eating a meal together
where each of us can feel at home
in listening and sharing.

For thirty years
your Son shared meals
in friendship with disciples and sinners,
and filled the multitude
by making certain
there was enough bread and wine for all.

And here we are gathered again
for a new meal of brotherhood.
Make your Spirit come upon us;
let him pry open our hearts
so that our love reaches everyone;
let him entrust to us
your nourishing Word and Presence.
May our words and works be reminders
of the death and resurrection of Jesus.
In this way, we anticipate

partaking in eternal life
when your Son will once again
drink the fruit of the vine
with all your children united together.

the freshness of new bread

2 Kings 4:42-44   *Matthew 14:13-21*
Isaiah 55:1-3   *Luke 9:11-17*
                     John 6:1-15

Eucharist/*Bread; Poverty.*

Be praised, Lord,
by parents
who set on the table each day
the fruit of their work:
bread of a life of contentment,
bread of a life full of difficulties,
so that their children might grow to adulthood.

People: Praise and glory be yours, forever.

Be praised, Lord,
by the poor man who each morning
must beg again for
the bread of tears and misery
and who sometimes tastes human compassion
in a loaf offered to him and shared.

People: Praise and glory be yours, forever.

Be praised, Lord,
by the militant
who offers his heart and life
so that his poor brothers
might one day taste
the bread earned by their own sweat.

People: Praise and glory be yours, forever.

Be praised, Lord,
by engineers and technicians
serving in poor nations

so that a more productive and better controlled earth
might produce a plentiful harvest of wheat, rice and beans.

People: Praise and glory be yours, forever.

Be praised, Lord,
for your presence
along side the fathers of families,
along side beggars, engineers and militants.
Your presence is mysterious and difficult to grasp,
and yet so strong and real
that we can derive life from it,
just as we live by eating bread.

People: Praise and glory be yours, forever.

Be praised, Lord,
by your Son, Jesus Christ,
in a way surpassed by no other.
He multiplied bread for the poor
and took his place at table with sinners.
Then on the night before his passion,
at that moment, in order to become the least among men,
he became bread pulled apart and broken,
passed from hand to hand and shared.

People: Praise and glory be yours, forever.

*   *   *

Lord, send your Spirit on this bread
so that it makes our hearts
poor and flexible,
open and sensitive
to every hunger and craving.

Lord, send your Spirit on your children
so that they are nourished with the life
of your Son who died for us;
so that they always have an unending supply
of this bread broken for each other.

Lord, send your Spirit on the men
who are famous throughout this world
and are influential in key decisions,
so that they mobilize to fight

against suffering and misery,
using all their resources of intelligence and love.

Lord, send your Spirit
on our fields,
on our farm workers and planters,
on those who make bread and all other food.

Finally, Lord, send your Spirit
into our hearts
to make our goals,
the goals of your Kingdom:

People: Our Father, who art in heaven. . . . .

eating with resentful people

Matthew 9:9-13
Offering/*Sin; Pardon.*

God wants only the sacrifice of forgiveness and mercy and takes
pleasure only in calling sinners to his table;
let us thank him, brothers, for inviting us here and let us in turn
call on our enemies to join us in offering together the sacrifice
of mutual forgiveness.

*   *   *

Let us pray in the name of our human brothers
that sin be removed from everyone:
from the rich who don't know
the joy of giving and receiving;
from governments which rely on power and money
to exert their influence in the world;
from husbands and wives who no longer have the strength to
forgive nor the humility to be sorry.

Let forgiveness be always open to them
and let them not give up hoping in a God
who has known from close up, without bitterness,
the coarseness of their evil.

People: Our peace when encountering you contains all
              forgiveness;

you who live near the Father
are pleading for us through your cross.

*   *   *

Let us pray for our human brothers
who quickly push aside
any well intentioned word,
who cover up their hesitations
by attempting to rationalize
and break the thrust of conversion
in their heart.
Let our charity find the necessary words
to stay with them
and share with them the power of the risen Lord
who will fashion them into new people.

People: Our peace when encountering you contains all
            forgiveness;
            you who live near the Father
            are pleading for us through your cross.

*   *   *

Let us pray for our human brothers,
victims resigned to injustice,
miserable men
whose powerlessness the rich exploit,
crushed men
whose life and body are at the mercy of bombs;
men robbed of their soul
by a materialistic civilization.

May God communicate with them.
God permitted
his Son to be victimized by sinners and the powerful.
May he forgive us
for forgetting each other,
and for being insensitive even to our mutual needs and desires.

People: Our peace when encountering you contains all
            forgiveness;
            you who live near the Father
            are pleading for us through your cross.

*   *   *

Let us pray for our human brothers
who lament their inability
to change the world
as they advocate unpopular causes.

May God reveal to them
that he too is powerless and foolish,
like his Son, Jesus Christ.
May we share that folly,
knowing that each failing person
and each slow moving change
are signs of life and signs of the Kingdom.

People: Our peace when encountering you contains all
forgiveness;
you who live near the Father
are pleading for us through your cross.

if the grain does not die

Matthew 13:24-43
Mark 4:26-34

Eucharist/*Planting; Delay;*
Slowness; Patience.

We praise you, Father of Jesus Christ,
for life shared
with plants, animals, men and your own Son;
for the productive earth which, from the beginning,
furnished milk and honey
for people who have lived here.

We thank you for harvests
which we reap from grain decomposed in the soil;
for the picking of fruit,
products of seeds which have died in the ground.

Your Church faces toward you,
with all those who, throughout the world,
search for the secrets of our soil
in order to proclaim your mystery:

People: Holy, holy, holy, the Lord is holy!
His love continues forever.

* * *

You are familiar with the laws of nature;
you know that each grain dies only to give birth to a new world.
That is why you were willing
to have your Word seeded
in the soil of indifference
and that your Son be planted
in ground cluttered with obstacles.

You are familiar with the laws of nature;
you know that each grain grows
only by passing through stages of delays and dormancy,
stages found in everything that grows,
or whenever something is born.
That is why you were willing
that your Son share in our human condition,
its slow-downs and its set-backs,
its ambiguities and its delays;
may your Word serve its apprenticeship
with the patience needed
for men to pay heed to your Word.
Your sowing has indeed resulted in a towering tree
and your Son never stops multiplying bread
as he did on the night before his death,
celebrating here on earth with his friends
his last meal,
made from our harvested bread
and our vintage wine.

* * *

Accept, Father, along with the sacrifice of your Son
the first fruits of our labor,
our joy in working with him in his kingdom on earth,
our desire to see happiness spread to all men.
You reunite us around this family table
as partakers in your bread and confidants in your thought;
grant that we work toward sowing seeds for a better world
with the same patience shown by your Son,
sensitive to all that is grand and beautiful

in our brothers and in creation,
respecting the delays and the slowness
which each of us accepts
in order to share in your Spirit.

And so let glory be given to you, Father,
in the unity of your Son and your Spirit,
for ever and ever.

People: Amen.

the strongest win out

Job 38:1-11
Mark 4:35-41

Agape/*Power; Suffering;*
Might; Failure.

Be praised, almighty God,
whom religious men have praised
since the beginning of time.
They recognized your power at work
in natural phenomena,
in the fantasy of seasons,
the birth of life,
the violence of the elements,
and the beauty of a flower!
Together with all men
throughout the universe
we add our voices
in the hymn to your power:

People: Holy is the Lord,
the God of the universe.
Heaven and earth are full of your glory!

But you did not wish to have
your power become an obstacle
between people and yourself;
instead of your power crushing people
and keeping them in fear,
you shared it with them.

They often abuse your power.
They devour it
as they issue indictments and condemnations.

Forgive them, Father,
and look rather
at the persevering effort of those
who try to make the world
a more fitting place for life
by creating machines which alleviate fatigue,
by harnessing the energy in elements.

Father, look upon this world
which reflects your image in an imperfect manner
without always being aware of it.
Your likeness is already present
in the hearts of the poorest of men.

People: Holy, holy, holy is the Lord,
              God of the universe.
              Heaven and earth are full of your glory!

                          *   *   *

And yet you keep another power secret
which you reveal to us.
In your Son, Jesus Christ,
your love was revealed
and we learned to recognize your power
in the face of a servant;
we have seen it weakened and struck down
by the blows of assassins.
During the storm, the apostles thought
it was silent and asleep;
our contemporaries believe it to be dead and ineffective,
for you display your might
only in the mystery of death;
you reveal your strength
only in the humble service of men.

People: Blessed is he who comes
              in the name of the Lord!

That is why, on the night before he died,
Jesus used just a bit of bread and wine

to represent his extreme weakness.
He confided them to his Church
so that, until the end of time,
around the most lowly of tables,
she commemorates to each person
the treasures of your glory and the riches of your power
by loving and serving that person.

People: Blessed is he who comes
         in the name of the Lord!

*   *   *

Father, send your Spirit on us
so that we might more easily recognize
your power in weakness,
your might in poverty,
your strength in suffering and death.

People: The Spirit of the Lord fills the universe.
         He knows every word, Alleluia.

Help us to follow the example of parents
who cherish their retarded child;
the example of young nuns
who show the sunrise to depressed old people;
the example of people lost in luxury and discontentment
who are forced to face a struggle
and are suddenly revived and restored to health.

People: The Spirit of the Lords fills the universe.
         He knows every word, Alleluia.

Help us to follow after our sick brothers and sisters
who serenely await their death
because they realize that you are the conqueror of death;
Give us strength to follow widows
who all of a sudden discover for themselves
a new life-giving strength.
Make us like all those among us
who every morning start working
all over again
so that their children might be happier.

People: The Spirit of the Lord fills the universe.
         He knows every word, Alleluia.

Father, look upon this power
displayed in unhappiness and failure;
see how we yearn to be joined to
this mysterious arrangement;
remember that your crucified Son
was once found in this condition
but is now dispensing glory and life
in your presence
for ever and ever.

People: Amen.

there's no holding back

Matthew 10:37-42
Luke 9:51-62

Agape/*Commitment; Acceptance;*
        Love.

Our hearts are rejoicing
because you alone, Father, love us
without condition and without holding back.
You love us more than
we could ever love ourselves.
You love us and take us more seriously
than any friend we ever knew.
You take our suffering so seriously
that you share in it completely;
you take our freedom so seriously
that you become its victim;
you take our refusal to love so seriously
that you do nothing to force us to give in to you.

We praise you,
Father of Jesus Christ,
for showing us your love and its serious nature
in the friendship our brothers show us
and in the commitments which they demand of us.
That is why we acclaim before you:

People: Holy, holy, holy is the Lord.
        His love endures forever.

You took your Son, Jesus Christ, seriously
and we recall his steady courage
in his decisive choices;
we recall too his quiet acceptance
of circumstances and persons.
He placed full confidence in your love
by being freed from every tradition
and disposed to every future event.
That is why his life and death
changed our life and death so drastically.
Being delivered over, once and for all, in a decision to love,
he never went back on his decision
and now knows
a total sharing of himself with you, Father.

People: We proclaim your death, Lord Jesus,
              we celebrate your resurrection,
              we await your coming in glory.

At this moment when such remembrances make us feel alive,
let your Spirit act in our hearts
so that we might make our commitment too
without holding back.
We are often disconcerted
because we have been obliged to take roads
which we would have avoided
had the choice been ours.
Rather than run the risk of human life and faith
we want to be reassured by that awful prudence
which teaches us to prefer ourselves
over you and our brothers.

May your Spirit teach us to get beyond
our ways of thinking of only the task at hand;
may he mobilize us for tasks
that surpass our powers
because so many of our brothers even now
expect from us the action which will free them.
May your Spirit be with us
and make us enter into the battle
against injustice and evil;
may he help us understand
that the poor and the crucified

are still among us;
may he invite us to join them
in order to become united to your Son, Jesus Christ.

People: Amen.

a prayer for people who never have anything to say

Matthew 11:25-30

Intercession/*Poverty; Simplicity;*
Sin; Humility.

We praise you,
Father, Lord of heaven and earth,
because you hide your presence
from wise and smug individuals
and reveal yourself
to those who expect everything
from you alone.
Come to our aid, God,
for it is not easy
to be so completely dependent on you.

People: Look at your Church, Lord,
and do not forget
that your poor have to stay alive.

Look at us — we are your Church
Remember to grace us with
your presence, strength —
vision + courage.
lead us Vooe
through to great discoveries

We praise you,
Father, Lord of heaven and earth,
because you chose as your people
the smallest group of all
so that your love would be plainly recognized
as a tremendous gift.
Come to our aid, God,
for it is not easy for us
not to be pompous and proud
as we forget
that you have chosen us

for the glory of your name
and the service of men. *others*

People: Look at your Church, Lord,
            and do not forget
            that your poor have to stay alive.

We praise you,
Father, Lord of heaven and earth,
because you remove the yoke of the law
from those whom you love
so that nothing might condemn
those whom you have reconciled.
Come to our aid, God,
for it is not easy
for us hardened sinners *complacent sinners*
to convert to your justice *(holiness)*
and find full comfort in your love.

People: Look at your Church, Lord,
            and do not forget
            that your poor have to stay alive.

We praise you,
Father, Lord of heaven and earth,
because you entrusted everything to Jesus
so that he might recognize
all that you asked of him.
He knows you not just through knowledge and wisdom
but also by sharing
the very same life with you.
He made himself poor among the poor;
everything he had he received from you.
When he mixed with sinners
he observed only the law of love.
Come to our aid, God, for it is not easy for us
to accept the bread and wine
offered by your Son
when we are so unwilling to partake in his poverty.

People: Look at your Church, Lord,
            and do not forget
            that your poor have to stay alive.

*   *   *

Send your Spirit on us, Father.
May our poverty *, our need, our dependency*
be like the poverty of Jesus,
open to your initiative,
enriched with your grace.
May our obedience
resemble the obedience of Jesus
in meekness and humility of heart.
Do not allow the poor and sinners *LOOK AT US*
to remain
excluded from your Kingdom forever.
Forgive the rich
for retaining their places so long.
Forgive the wise
for making statements
which are unintelligible to the ~~ordinary man.~~ *its ordinary people.*
And finally, reassemble us
in unity and love,
in the service of our ~~brothers~~ *+ sisters*
and for the glory of your name,
through Jesus Christ, your Son, our Lord.
People: Look at your Church, Lord,
       and do not forget
       that your poor have to stay alive.

hold out your hand and don't pull it back

Luke 10:25-37
Eucharist/*Love*

Father, be praised
for the love you witness toward men
in always taking the initiative in loving them.
People: For his great love is without end!
You have given us your Spirit.
You placed love in the hearts of men
so that husbands love their wives

and parents love their children,
so that the old are reborn
when we smile at them
and the poor find security in the friendship
their brothers show them.
Extend our hands
beyond the easy limits we set for ourselves.

People: For his great love is without end.

You have given us freedom
and you know how we abuse it.
We exclude when we should be accepting;
we condemn rather than forgive.

*   *   *

That is why, Father,
we ask you to forget our errors
and remember the charity expressed by your Son.
He remained in your love;
he did everything he could for his brothers;
and he loved them and even died for them.
We recognized your love in him
on the evening when he reunited his friends
for the last time
and gave himself totally to them.

—For your death and resurrection,

People: Glory to you, O Lord.

—For your love for men and your love for the Father

People: Glory to you, O Lord.

—For your Spirit who dwells in our hearts,

People: Glory to you, O Lord.

*   *   *

We recognize your Spirit at work
in the love which people show toward each other,
in their efforts for more social justice,
in their attempts to bring about international peace,
in the human family's tremendous expectations
which urge people to change the face of the earth
so that the rhythm of your life is actually lived here.

People: Lord, send your Spirit
who renews the face of the earth.

We offer to you, Father,
with your Son's love,
the warm unity of our group.
our faithfulness to the Church throughout the world,
our love for people having real needs.
Purify our love;
may our love be more like your Son's love
so that we can realize the promise of your Kingdom.
Renew our hearts
so that all of us, just as we are,
with different faces and different souls,
prepare together
for your coming among us
forever and ever.

People: Amen.

finding god in a human face

Proverbs 9:1-6   John 17:11-19
John 6:51-59   1 John 4:11-18
Thanksgiving/*Transcendence; Immanence;
                Table.*

Be praised, Holy God!

No thought can encompass you
and yet you make the universe your dwelling place
and you make us your people.

No one can measure the depths of your wisdom,
and yet your wisdom is friendly to man
and teaches us
to call them: Brothers;
and to call you: Father.

Your Spirit is more subtle
than breath or wind;
no one knows where it comes from
or where it is going.

But your Spirit does penetrate our human hearts,
and though we begin as strangers,
the Spirit unites us
as we come to love and understand each other
in a deeper, richer way.

You accept our hospitality,
and your familiar footstep awakens the whole house;
you are the one who sets
the dinner table;
you fill our cups,
and you are seated among us.
Yes, you are close to us, God of strength;
you are nearby, God of mystery!

You separate us from the world,
but you do not wish to take us out of the world;
you tell us to love you,
but the only face we see that belongs to you
is the face of our brothers.

*   *   *

Recognize in the dinner guests
the hesitant bearers of your light,
the fragile witnesses of your life;
make their faith grow
so that whatever events are in store for them,
whether good times or bad,
may be filled with your love
and your truth.

so much of the bumper crop is dumped in the sea

Matthew 15:21-28
Mark 7:24-30
Penitential Prayer/*Bumper Crop; Universalism;
                    Sufficiency.*

Lord, you multiplied for us
bread and wine

with such abundance
that our baskets are still full;
But we refuse to allow this overabundance of crops
to be used to feed the poorest of our brothers.
Change our hearts, Lord,
so that we give less consideration
to our hunger for profit;
help us be more sensitive to the poor in our country,
and the people of other lands.

People: Let us not forget the cry of anguish
          which rises up before you.

You have given us a segment of truth
which we learn through our science and our culture;
and we try to make this small segment the monopoly and secret
of one social class or one nation;
we refuse to share our secrets
with our less fortunate brothers.
Make us understand, Lord,
that each truth bears fruit
when it is exchanged and shared.

People: Let us not forget the cry of anguish
          which rises up before you.

Lord, your creative love has called us
to be your guests
at this meal of divine life and grace;
but we have forgotten your initiative
and we have made your meal
a privileged, "by invitation only" affair.
We have lost sight of the fact
that very many places remain unoccupied;
many of those invited do not come
because living with us is not very attractive to them.
Remind us, Lord,
that you have died for all men
and that it is up to us
to see that everyone is able
to celebrate in unity
the memorial of your Passover.

People: Let us not forget the cry of anguish
          which rises up before you.

You were not afraid, Lord,
to enter into a foreign land
to meet there those invited to your Kingdom;
you stripped yourself of your Jewish privileges
to get close to very humble, despised people.
Give us, Lord,
disgust for our monopolies
which feed our proud spirits
and give us the desire for the long reeducation
we will have to undergo
as we learn to share and dialogue.

People: Let us not forget the cry of anguish
which rises up before you.

for you and for many

Mark 7:1-23

Offering/*Sacrifice; Pure/Impure;
Love; Unity.*

Brothers,
before we gather around this altar
to commemorate Christ's sacrifice,
let us ask him to purify our intentions
so that the Father will not turn away
as we offer him our lives.

Together with all our human brothers
who, in trying to be faithful to their human condition,
reject our prayers and sacrifices;
let us strip our religion
of all hypocrisy
so that our prayer and our offering
may rise up to the invisible and mysterious God
whom we cannot fully name
or reduce to ideas or images.

People: Yes, love is so much better
than the best of sacrifices.

Together with men of all times
who believe that their human life

derives its value
from the magic in sacred rites,
let us recognize that we depend on the Father
and let us offer to him a spiritual sacrifice.
May our prayer and sacrifice
rise up to the Father
who, through our prayers,
holds our lives in his hands.

People: Yes, love is so much better
than the best of sacrifices.

Together with all our Christian brothers
from whom we are separated
by our selfishness and our divisiveness,
and before people reject the Church
because of her inability to bring about unity,
let us offer to God
a Eucharist of true reconciliation
because in God is found the secret for communion.

People: Yes, love is so much better
than the best of sacrifices.

Together with members of the People of God,
with the pope, with bishops of the whole world,
let us be in tune with the Church
throughout all the world,
so that our prayer and our offering
and our concern for all local churches
are carried up to God.

People: Yes, love is so much better
than the best of sacrifices.

Together with the Holy Spirit
who knows the deepest secrets of our hearts,
and who inspires us
to find meaning in all things,
let us offer to God our hope
and the hope that all creation has
that one day the universe will be
in the hands of God's children.

People: Yes, love is so much better
than the best of sacrifices.

a priestly people

Hebrews 12:22-25

Psalm/*Solidarity; Mediation;*
        Universalism; Jews.

Be praised, Father of Jesus Christ.
We are here in your presence in your likeness;
we yearn to live with our brothers
in a humanity marked by contentment and brotherhood.
Each of us becomes who we are
only through the influence every other man has on us.

We give you thanks
and we acknowledge how indebted we are
to the love our parents gave us,
to the expertise of our teachers,
to the discretion of friends,
to the clear thinking of our leaders.

Someone has come into prominence among us;
he became
what we made him become:
his mother's womb formed him
and his father's occupation did too;
he was affected by friendship with hardened sinners
and quick success with the crowds;
the strong hostilities in our hearts
and the nails in his hands and feet
took away his life.
He was called Jesus, the name
which men had given to him.

Consider how he responds to what he has received;
we who made him what he is
must in turn acknowledge
what we owe to him:
we are his brothers in divine life.
So that this exchange would be perfect
and his mediation complete,
Jesus made his body
the possession of mankind,

the heart of all religion,
the altar of spiritual worship.

*   *   *

Be praised, Father.
You have placed your image in humanity;
men yearn to live beyond today's frontiers
in a universe of peace and harmony.
And each nation becomes what it must be
through the influence all other nations have on it.

We are grateful
for all that our nations
owe to each other
in the exchange of goods,
ideas, scientific discoveries,
in the difficult meetings
around conference tables,
in treaties for peace
and mutual assistance.

A group of people has come into prominence among us;
in order to transmit to all nations
the Word which that group heard,
and in order to make sure you were listening
to the cry of other nations in search of you,
that nation offered you a cult of praise
in the name of all nations;
they lived a life of holiness,
made up of everything that man receives from you.

Here we are before you, Father,
reliving what Israel experienced.
As we live among all kinds of people,
we are receiving from them
everything that you want us to be.
We seek to give meaning
to their effort to arrive at a greater brotherhood.
We attempt to share in
their woeful complaints of sadness
and their ecstatic outbursts of joy.

We also give you thanks
for receiving our concern with such understanding

and for accepting it as the spiritual sacrifice
of the priesthood which you have invested in us
through your Son, Jesus Christ.

People: Amen.

you have planted the word

Mark 7:31-37

Thanksgiving/*Communication; Word.*

Father, be praised
for the gift of hearing and for the word
which allows us to communicate
with the world and with men, our brothers,
and for all that reaches our ears:
the murmur of a stream, a gust of wind,
birds singing, and the entire symphony of the world.

Be praised for the noise of engines and rockets,
symbols of a universe
which man is gradually controlling and transforming,
for the sounds which the solo artist
orchestrates in praising you,
and for the joyful shouts of men.

Be praised
for the tremendous privilege of human language:
for the jibber-jabbering of tiny tots,
their first communication
with the world of people and things;
for dialogue in marriage,
source of intimate sharing and mutual joy;
for brothers reaching out to each other
as they slowly build a better world
according to your image.

Be praised
for the gift of Jesus Christ, your Living Word
to men of all times;
for the mission which you give to us

to announce your message of joy,
and for the building up of the Kingdom.

*   *   *

In memory of the gift of your Word to the world,
and in union with Jesus, dead and risen,
we present our continuing efforts
to give ear to the events of each day.
Accept the poverty of our dialogues
and our difficulties in communicating fully
with our brothers.

*   *   *

And now, God of warmth and understanding,
we know you accept the arduous unraveling
of the dialogue between men
and you respect our sluggishness and our hesitations
in converting to your Word.
Through your Spirit, bolster our courage
as we struggle.
Over the roar of cannons may we superimpose
a harmony which respects persons
and constructs peace.
May we challenge adults to be more attentive
to the cries of young people
who are struggling to bring more reality and brotherhood
into the world.
May we become, as you are,
capable of interpreting every language.

*   *   *

May your love break down in us
barriers of prejudice,
egotism which dooms dialogue to failure,
cold wars which are part of our way of life,
faint heartedness which conceals your presence
from the world.
May the desire grow in us to speak your Word
despite the difficulties we experience
as we speak about you to modern man.
Teach us to talk with you

and to pray with you as we should,
through Jesus Christ,
who is the way that we communicate with you.

People: Amen.

his speech impediment has been removed

Mark 7:31-37
Psalm/*Speechless; Word;*
       Prayer.

We should praise you
with words that have the force of the wind,
with words of prophetic caliber,
with words which no one forgets
and even the deaf would be able to understand.

We should sing to you
with words heavier than silence,
with words as simple as love,
with words which you would not forget
and your Word could set to music.

We should praise you
with words as piercing as the cries of the poor,
with words lyrical as a poem,
with words which you could pronounce
to transform the world.

We should pray to you
with the naive words of a happy-go-lucky toddler,
with words pronounced seriously like in an oath,
with words that are not quickly answered by you
because we realize that what we say to you
is merely an echo of your words to us.

We should cry out to you
with hostile words having sharp edges,
with heated two-fisted words,

with angry words which force us
to pace the floor all night long.

But we manage to say something
so that our words might charm your ear
with insignificance and lowliness;
we cool off our words
so that they do not burn our lips
as we give ourselves the privilege of lying.

God of mutes and gossips,
you exist without being named;
you existed before words;
God of silence and words,
why do you wish your name
spoken and proclaimed in human words?

after the revolution is over

Mark 12:38-44
Luke 16:19-31

Agape/*Poverty; Recognition.*

Be praised, Father of Jesus Christ.
You are a God like no one ever knew before,
a God, humble and poor, attentive to each man;
we would have no words to speak to you
had not Jesus, our brother, with our own words
become your word and your expression.

People: Christ is among us, alleluia! (three times)

He shared our miserable condition
in which the poor are manipulated
toward greater profit-making by the rich
and the ordinary man is despised by learned men.
Jesus saw how men usually ignored their brothers
or dominated them.
He did not find much love, justice and freedom among us.

People: Christ is among us, alleluia! (three times)

He took upon himself all of this insupportable misery,
this universal sin, this revolt rising up in the hearts
of those who cannot escape
the mirages of our fleeting horizons;
he began to dream with us
about new men who would get to know each other
and would love each other.

People: Christ is among us, alleluia! (three times)

He kept alive his dream about a world
where there would be no more broken homes,
and no more soldiers killing each other,
where the unemployed would be quickly hired,
where children could eat
until their stomachs were full,
where prisons would release
those jailed for being outspoken,
where sleep each night would no longer be
just a way to escape from life.

People: Christ is among us, alleluia! (three times)

But Jesus ate the last crumb
of the bread of our misery;
he drank every drop of our poverty
because he died
before his ridiculous ideal
had a chance to take shape.
Be praised, Father of Jesus Christ;
you gave to our brother this new human family
for which he had dreams
and for which he died.

People: Christ is among us, alleluia! (three times)

Father, see our weakness:
man is still very far from loving his brother;
we shrug off with indifference
the outcries of the poor around us.
but we know that love is possible
and that love is a gift from you.
Send the Spirit of your Son upon us
to teach us to make the effort
to recognize the dignity in each person we meet.

People: Christ is among us, alleluia!

Send us the Spirit of your Son.
Bless those who have accepted the challenge
of reminding us constantly
about the demands of your love.
Bless those who rebel
against injustice and oppression
as they strive to build a world
more suited for human life.   *—Declaration—*
Bless those who understand
that we must live human poverty
as Jesus did.

People: Christ is among us, alleluia!

We praise you, Father of Jesus Christ,
for your work of unity amid all divisions,
for your love amid all our hatred,
for your Son who is inconspicuous
among all the poor in the world,
for your Spirit who prepares our hearts
for the Kingdom which is approaching
and will last forever and ever.

People: Amen.

as you gaze into my eyes

Mark 10:46-52

Thanksgiving/*Blindness; Light.*

Father,
we would have always remained blind men
if you had not sent your Son
to open our eyes;
he lived entirely for others;
he extended his hand so that others would grasp it;
his eyes searched constantly to catch the gaze of others.
Through him,
you wanted to take us by the hand
and open our eyes for us,

so that we might also extend our hand to our brothers,
and that together we might make you visible to people;
God, you are alive and hidden.

That is why, in the faith
which you have given us to share,
we make the decision
to witness the light brought to us by your Son,
his birth in our human condition
and his life given for us on the cross.
We thank you for raising him from the dead
and making him be alive to us
at each moment in the Spirit
until one day he will reunite us in your presence
to unveil before our eyes your glory
which our faith even now tries to grasp.
We ask you, Father, to open our eyes
and make us discover your presence
in the universe and in our brothers.
Please send your Spirit upon us
so that we might live the very life of Christ;
then men will be able to discover
your presence in us.

noise and shouting; shouting and the word

Matthew 23:1-12

Agape/ *Word; Teaching; Lying.*

We praise you, Father of Jesus Christ,
for the words which you place on our lips.
Each word puts flesh on our thoughts;
we express our word and immediately the world changes.
Our word discloses the secret of the world around us
and invokes its mystery.
Once a word is spoken, nothing can take it back.
Our word is serious when it gives descriptions.
It is jovial when said in jest.

People: Your word, Lord, is truth
and your law is deliverance.

Your Word, Father, has taken on the sound of our voice
in Jesus Christ, your Son.
Your Word has really touched our hearts
because it is good news.
More disconcerting
than the words spoken by rabbis,
more truthful
than the words spoken by philosophers,
this word unmasks all lies and deceptions
because it is The Word
which gives deep meaning to every statement.

Your Word, Father, has surpassed our half-truths.
It has been put to death
by casuists and pseudo-intellectuals;
it has become the word beyond death,
spoken from that place where nothing can gag it.
Your Word continues to accomplish its mission
by giving everything a name and a meaning.
That is why our bread can become Christ's body
and our wine, his blood and covenant.

People: Your word, Lord, is truth
and your law is deliverance.

This is the reason why apostles taken from among men
can succeed in being the messengers of your word,
and are received in all humility.
That is why those who have been given the task of teaching
can make discoveries in the mysteries
of the life and destiny of mankind
and can bring the word of reassurance
to those who are doubting.

That is why men and women can hear your word
in the silence of their hearts,
why events in life also become words
which pose questions to us
and greatly confuse us,
why people can dialogue
with greater depth each day
even if their language is hesitant

and their responses always remain mere questions
for the next day's dialogue.

People: Your word, Lord, is truth
              and your law is deliverance.

Grant that in hearing these diverse
and yet harmonious words,
the entire family of man
might one day be captivated
by the contemplation of your glory
in each person and each thing.
for ever and ever.

People: Amen.

from the seed of martyrs

Luke 21:5-19
Agape/*Witness; War; Peace.*

We praise you, Father,
because people who believe
try to build peace
amid the noises of war;
because people who believe
try to bring about sharing
amid famine and distress;
because people who believe
try to proclaim justice
amid the profit gains of those in power.

Be joyful, Father,
to rediscover your image and likeness
in their decision to construct
a city of peace and brotherhood,
having no painful cries, no tears,
where you will be all in all,
acknowledged by every man
without exception.

                              *   *   *

We now recall
pacifists forced to appear

before war councils,
prophets who spoke the truth
and were murdered by the inquisition,
people who had a passion
for dislogue and innovation
and were misunderstood by the power structure.

We recall
your Son, Jesus Christ, among us.
His death gave meaning
to the sacrifice of prophets and martyrs.
Your Son's oblation pleased you, Father,
and you raised him up.
Accept in that same sacrifice
the offering of the victims of war and famine,
injustice and oppression.
May their sacrifice not be in vain.
Let it prepare us for a better world,
the sign of the kingdom where you will celebrate
the eternal banquet with us.

ordinary for an agape (I)

Various Prayers/*Prayer; Word.*

1. *Opening Prayer*

Father, you have called before you
Jesus Christ, your Son, our brother,
so that he would bring your word
to all men whom he loved.
We are gathered together today
to be, in our own way, authentic witnesses
of that humanity which he loved.
May we follow him with full devotion
to merit being about to speak to you in his name,
with Jesus Christ, your Son, our Lord.

People: Amen.

2. *Conclusion of the Liturgy of the Word*

Your word spoken to us today
remains mysterious to us, Father;
it is so demanding
that we protect ourselves
from listening to it.
May we make a firm decision
to believe in your word,
to open our hardened hearts to your invitation
in order to live by your Spirit.
Make our faith grow; lead us to truth.
Come, Lord, and do not delay!

3. *Conclusion of the Prayer of the Faithful*

Father,
men have so often heard it said
that you are near to those who call upon you.
But their mouths are dried out from calling out to you
and their shout becomes despair or rebellion.
We realize, Father, that your response to our prayer
is made known to us
through what we do and what we touch.
May we not continue to be deaf

to what you are saying to us
through the grace of your Spirit.

People: Amen.

4. *Before the Kiss of Peace*

We break this bread with one another
as we realize, with Jesus Christ, our Lord,
that we cannot partake of this bread
without also handing over our body and our life.

5. *Concluding Prayer*

Lord,
you have fed us with Word and Bread.
Now give us that faith
which opens us to the needs of our times
and makes us ready to get involved.
Only then will your word become tasty for us,
and your bread, a slice of eternal life.

People: Amen.

ordinary for an agape (II)

Various Prayers/*Prayer.*

1. *Opening Prayer*

Father,
your Son, Jesus Christ, has made his break with us,
like a dead man who leaves his friends and family.
But you call us together today
to fill this void with your Spirit,
and to teach us how to cope
with the absence of Jesus.
This is similar to your way of existing:
you are present to us and hidden at the same time.
Give us eyes
which go beyond what is visible,
hearts which are willing to love
even when it means losing our lives.
Through Jesus Christ, your Son, our Lord.

People: Amen.

2. *Conclusion of the Liturgy of the Word*

You are the word
which rises up from our hearts;
you are the word
which our lips pronounce;
you pray in us
with your Spirit
while our minds are sluggish;
teach us to pray
by learning to be silent in your presence.

3. *Conclusion of the Prayer of the Faithful*

Father, hear this long list of intentions and petitions
which are really our outbursts of impatience.
It is not possible
for death to triumph over life,
lies over the truth.
It is not possible
for the poor to remain always hungry.
The outcries we make in prayer
are like shouting out of a deep well
because we lack the courage
to do what we should to alleviate these problems.
We ask you, Father, to be patient with us;
do not give up on our faith.
May your Spirit in our hearts
inspire and support our activity.

4. *Concluding Prayer*

Through your word and your Spirit, Father,
you have recreated us
in the image of your Son.
Continue to form in us
this image of love and forgiveness;
Make us concerned for the poor
and advocates of freedom;
and may your Son quickly fulfill all our dreams,
for ever and ever.

People: Amen.

may he live forever

Thanksgiving/*Baptism; Child; Family;*
Catechumenate; Birth.

Lord,
you are the creator of everything beautiful and loveable.
We thank you for N __ __ __.
to whom N__ __ __ and N __ __ __ have given life.

Source of all that breathes,
give health to this child;
Source of all beauty,
give him sensitivity and imagination.

May his mind progress
in the discovery of truth.
May his hands serve
to transform the world
May his eyes never be closed
to the misery around him.
May his heart be open and generous.

We thank you, Lord,
in the name of his parents,
for whom N __ __ __ has become
the living sign of their love.
May he always be
a source of unity for them,
in good times and in difficult times.
May N __ __ __ and N __ __ __ have health and courage
each day as they fashion N __ __ __ into full
Christian adulthood.

(We thank you, Lord,
because we are united in the joy of his brothers and sisters
who will share their family life with him
and will make him their companion
as they discover life together.)

*   *   *

And now, Lord,
may we not be the only ones who experience this happiness;
keep in mind all married couples;
may their struggle against selfishness

not be in vain.
Give them, and us too,
your strength to be faithful lovers;
may our children come to recognize you
as their loving Father;
may we give orphans and abandoned children
a home and a warm welcome
so that these unfortunate children
might see in our sharing
the larger family of man.

Inspire all families to be faithful to your word
so that in listening to you,
children will discover their calling in life
and be ready to serve others.

You make the living waters flow.
Grant that this child,
who has been buried with your Son
in the waters of Baptism,
might now rise to newness of life;
help him make his journey toward you
as he loves and struggles,
together with Christ, the new Adam,
in the friendship of the Holy Spirit,
in union with the members of your Church.

life being born from life

Thanksgiving/*Baptism; Child; Life;*
             Family; Birth.

We praise you, Father of Jesus Christ.
You are the source of life
and you fill us with joy
as we renew life today.
You are present within every act of love,
so that all love might produce happiness
and the gift of life.

Be praised
for this child, for the miracle of his prenatal development

and his birth into life,
for his first look of recognition
and his first smile,
for his conquest of the world
which he is already undertaking
with his reaching gestures and his crying.
For you decided
that in following your Son's example,
he truly shares the condition of men
in encounter, in brotherhood,
and in conquest of the world.

Be praised.
You decided to give
an even richer meaning
to the love N ___ ___ ___ and I share and to our parenthood
by making N ___ ___ ___
a member of your family.

*   *   *

Remember us, Father.
Bless the responsibilities that we take on
and bless the courage of those
who help us to fulfill them.
Remember our parents
and those who have helped us
with their concern and friendship
when N ___ ___ ___ was born.

Remember the real world of men,
children without parents,
and homes without children.

May your kingdom come, Father,
for ever and ever.
Amen.

light being born from light

Matthew 5:14
Holding the Candle/*Baptism; Light.*

N ___ ___ ___, receive this lighted candle;
may it always be

the sign of your entirely new outlook
which is discovering beauty in everything you see;
the sign of the smile
which lights up your face
and brings joy to those around you.
You will be familiar with the weakness of people
and their difficult life:
you will share in their restlessness
and carelessness.
Remain among us always
as solid as this candle,
luminous and warm as its flame.

And when you own light will grow dim,
when its flame will be less alive,
remember that you have entered into a world
which looks toward the future,
for Jesus Christ, our Lord,
is the light of the world;
he does not fail those
whom he takes into his love.

praying that their love will grow

Canticle of Canticles 2:8-16   *John 15:9-16*
Romans 8:31-39   *1 John 4:7-12*
Ephesians 5:25-33

Agape/*Marriage; Love; Family.*

It is in the name of N __ __ __ and N __ __ __
that all of us here today have gathered together
to give you thanks,
Father of Jesus Christ, our Father.

*   *   *

Because they have stepped forward,
they are committing themselves to each other
and they are giving themselves to each other
as never before;
they know today what your Son decided

when he delivered himself over
through bread and wine.

Because they are bound to each other,
they face their life together with freedom,
sharing responsibility for their future,
in a very human way.

Because they are in love with each other,
they learned
that tenderness gives life a surprisingly delightful meaning,
and they joyfully share in the happiness which you experience
in loving people.

Because they have tasted some happiness,
they know that love is stronger than time,
and that hope is always reborn
whenever problems arise;
And so they are renewing their faith
in the resurrection of your Son, Jesus Christ.

*   *   *

Send your Spirit among us
so that the parents of N __ __ __ and N __ __ __
accept with serenity
the departure of their child
and find in the newlyweds
the reawakening of their own love.

Send your Spirit among us;
may he help us to a deeper sharing
in the sorrow of spouses
who are separated by death or infidelity.

Send your Spirit among us
so that he may be present
in the plans N __ __ __ and N __ __ __ are making.

And each time that this love will be renewed,
let your Spirit reinkindle them again and again,
like fire in their hearts,
like sunlight in their eyes,
in order to carry their love beyond the grave.

And when this love will bring a child into the world,
may your Spirit be present to them again;

may their tenderness be renewed
in the openness they show as a couple toward others.

Send your Spirit among us
so that the bread which we eat together
and the mystical wine which we drink
will bring to us all
the love and friendship of each person here,
along with your love, Father,
in Jesus Christ, your Son, our Lord.

source of community

Agape/*Saying Farewell to Each Other.*

We praise you, Lord!
We came together some time ago,
weighed down by our worries,
our minds full of questions and problems.
Look how we have become renewed persons,
full of hope and love
for all those whom we will touch;
your work is in our hands;
your name is on our lips.
We praise you, Lord!

People: O Lord, our God,
how great is your name
in the entire universe.

We praise you, Lord!
We have met each other
whose life history we knew nothing about.
And here we are about to face our future together,
ready to rid ourselves of our security blankets
so that your gospel will inspire tomorrow's world.
We praise you, Lord!

People: O Lord, our God,
how great is your name
in the entire universe.

We praise you, Lord!
We have gotten to know

and care for each other
and we serve each other's needs.
We have discovered our mutual shortcomings
and our prejudices.
Here we are ready to serve without being self imposing,
to help others without humiliating them
so that love transforms our cities,
and forgiveness continues to bring our urban areas
back to life.
We praise you, Lord!

People: O Lord, our God,
             how great is your name
             in the entire universe.

We praise you, Lord!
We have heard
the word of Jesus
who has given us a chance to perceive more clearly
who you are and who you are not!
Here are our voices
which will carry your voice to our brothers
of every language, race and country.
Let not your word be said in vain,
but may it plant the seeds of faith and love;
and in this way,
what you have begun to do among us
will be accomplished;
and when your day will come,
you will reap
what you have sown in our hearts.
We praise you, Lord!

People: O Lord, our God,
             how great is your name
             in the entire universe.

We praise you, Lord!
If we have succeeded in knowing you better
and loving you more,
and if you have renewed our spirit
and rediscovered our fervor,
all this has happened to us
as we remember your Son, Jesus Christ,
his life among us,

the table he has set for his friends,
his death and resurrection.

People: O Lord, our God,
how great is your name
in the entire universe.

Send your Spirit on us;
may he strengthen us in your truth
and strip us of our quick conclusions.
May we find him
in our trials and failures,
in our moments of happiness and joy.
May he be revealed to us
in our brothers and in our elders,
in believers and unbelievers;
and may he make our lives
truly pleasing to you
in Jesus Christ, your Son, our Lord.

People: Amen.

surviving

Offering/*Funeral; Death; Hope; Alone.*

Father, we are utterly poor
before you
because we have lost
a father, a husband, a friend, a brother.
We are now experiencing for ourselves
the loneliness and emptiness
which he knew in his agony,
the loneliness and emptiness
experienced by your Son on the cross.

Father, we are very confident
before you,
for with N __ __ __ in your presence,
a small part of us
is united to you
and already lives with you
for ever and ever.
Amen.

you favor them over us

Thanksgiving/*Funeral; Death.*

We give you thanks,
Father of Jesus Christ,
because Jesus is alive
and so are all those
whom you have entrusted to him.
He conquered death for us,
for us and for all our departed loved ones.
We know that you are now showing greater affection
toward them, than you show toward us;
and you continue to love them
because you inspire us to love them
with a love that comes from you.
We have noticed on their faces
how they resemble your Son,
and we know that death cannot erase this likeness,
for you are life,
for ever and ever.

People: Amen.

by paul guerin

It would be useless for me to pretend to be impartial and objective in my comments. The preceeding pages contain prayers which are a kind of pleading: the pleading of a friend; the pleading of a Christian delighted to use these formulas in praying; and the pleading of a catechist deeply convinced that it is possible to pray community prayers (this certainly includes eucharistic prayers) which are completely modern and, at the same time, "radically" traditional.

I am certain that these prayers will not please everyone. In fact they can be very threatening to the reader. The prayers reflect the sentiments of the community which created them. This was a group of thirty priests from every continent. They lived together for one year and celebrated the Eucharist each Sunday with several laymen.

These prayers cannot and should not appeal to everyone. And they are in no way meant to be the last word in liturgy. They are more an incentive rather than the model, more a leaven than the baked loaf. This book does not fear competition. Competition is invited. It is my sincere hope that responsible liturgists will encourage Christian communities to be daring and creative, following the example of our creative forefathers, especially in the Eucharist where the essence of prayer is found.

Because for centuries we have been accustomed to just one Roman canon, we have only lately started to discover the wide variety of ancient eucharistic prayers. If the Eucharist is to be prayed throughout the world, cultural differences should then be recognized: Mozarabic wordiness along with Roman-Ambrosian severity, Gallican spontaneity with the classicism of Antioch, the simplicity of Alexandria (I am thinking mainly of Serapion) along with the wild outbursts of Ethiopia (what a rare, imaginative liturgy!).

The three new official Roman canons give us a small introduction to this necessary pluralism. But these three formulations are not modern prayers except in so far as they are truly universal in their petitions. Actually, the new canons are good neopatristic reconstructions. This comment is not said out of disdain. By going back to ancient prayers we are taking an indispensable pedagogical step. A baby has to learn to crawl before walking.

It really does not matter that the new canons are neopatristic and out-dated, and are therefore not very appealing to our modern tastes. Authentic faith has always been expressed through the religious sentiment of a particular era: people spontaneously thought of God as the Supreme Being; he was "in the heavens" and the angelic multitude rightfully occupied the vast distance which separated the Creator from his earthly creation. Earth was of little value when compared to heaven; human life was regarded as only a return to the fatherland: Jesus came down and then went up again; he "passed over" from this world.

This classic "religious" perspective (the profane and the sacred) required a particular corresponding attitude in the people. This attitude, reflective worship, required people to perform their duties before God by adoring, offering, expiating, and by "bringing human actions onto the divine sphere" (Bouyer). Jesus became High Priest; the Incarnation did not suppress the gap between God and man, but merely provided a bridge.

The old mentality was therefore "religious" and "worship oriented" as I have very briefly indicated. But it should be recognized that in these primitive prayers this mentality was indeed the expression of faith. We are too quick to overlook the *tension* between the spontaneous religious sensitivity of the people of a certain era and their faith in God's historic interventions in Jesus Christ. When belief in an incarnate God emphasized the sacral-profane distinction, following St. Paul's invitation to make one's entire life a sacrifice, then it was of considerable importance to worship at fixed hours. This is how our fathers reconciled their faith, which desacralized and decultualized, with their religious sensitivity which sacralized and cultualized.

I do not find this tension deplorable. *I think it is admirable.* It is this tension which creates the beauty of Byzantine, Antiochian and Alexandrinian anaphora. Even our old Roman canon kept its pagan vocabulary in the way it addressed the Father of Jesus Christ.

Faith cannot exist in a vacuum any more than can the kerygma (the proclamation of Salvation in Jesus Christ) when in its purest form. The kerygma immediately adopts the categories and expressions of the culture of the day. The praying faith is dressed up in the religious sensitivity and the connatural, ritualistic behavior of the group celebrating the prayer. A eucharistic prayer is well balanced when there is no denial of the articles of faith, represented in the symbolic ritual, and when there is an expression of the sensitivity of the community which is here and now celebrating these mysteries.

The very first thing that impressed me about this collection of prayers is that they speak to us in our own language and strike a chord favorable to our modern tastes. I will not conceal my hope that these community prayers will be received as a challenging call for truly contemporary eucharistic prayers.

*   *   *

Is it possible to explain the scope of the modern sensitivity which is expressed in the formulas of this book?

Faith in God is not a self-evident statement of fact which can stand, so to speak, by itself. It is a struggling faith which has experienced and still experiences a twinge of unbelief. It is a faith which has discovered God only after passing through a dark night.

A better explanation might be that faith in God is revealed through a mystical experience which is marked by a personal and incommunicable certainty about God's presence. There is no rationalizing. Faith simply attests: "He is here. He speaks. He gives Himself."

God is the luminous cloud: inaccessible and close by, mysterious and real, unfathomable and within reach. John of the Cross gives a good explanation of these themes which are characteristic of mystical faith.

This faith refuses to leave Egypt or Canaan to venture into Horeb. *God is among men* in their words, their hopes, their loves and their thirst for freedom. This is what is meant by experiencing the deeply religious dimensions of the human condition. Within the person who loves, who struggles and is hopeful —and this is not trite—there is a vibration which comes from afar, sort of like a mysterious chord. Our modern faith therefore assumes a sacred dimension, a religious sense. Here the sacred is not looked for in the nature of the cosmos, but in the sacred and religious aspect of man, the sacred context of man. It is not the sacredness of terror (fear of the recesses of my own interior darkness), but the sacredness of giving: the infinite resonance of my love, my hope, my commitment. All of this comes from afar and transcends me. Modern Christians express their faith through the sacredness of man, the sacredness of personal relationships and the sacredness of commitment within a community. Another facet of modern spirituality is the desire for a deep bond between human experience and spiritual experience. Human experience is the experience of freedom and responsibility. This experience is inalienable in two senses of the word. We cannot renounce the meaning given in theological explanations of the past. Spiritual experience is experiencing Him Who is Completely Other, who fills us, the God who is the source of our deepest being. Any attempt to reconcile these two experiences must avoid both concurrence and annexation. In this book, the reader will find a balance characterized by these expressions: "Friend and Father, Creator who gives himself, Creator who shares." The Father is described as a Father who is in no way paternalistic, but rather a Father who confides in people what so totally captures his heart: brotherhood, concern for the poor, making the universe more human.

Here we see modern religious sentiment bordering on the genuine faith based on the gospels: the Father loves us without being condescending and reveals himself as the God of Jesus Christ. This God who no longer seems comfortable amid smoking thuribles shows a yearning for meetings (by this I mean any and every fraternal gathering); he allows concerned people to call meetings which often deal militantly with issues; this God seems to tune in well to peace movements; he is surely the humble, dejected, passionate, suffering God who can be seen in flesh and blood in our streets.

He is a God, as Bonhoeffer says, *in transcendence,* and this means *the transcendence of love.* He loves more than anyone else and in his way of loving he goes beyond the limits set up by our most daring daydreams. His real power is revealed in lowering himself, and he finds a home with people who are most insignificant and least respected.

God's glory for us in modern times is human success measured by going beyond the limits of self, until man encounters Him who is the source of this need to get continually beyond self.

And this is the reason why, not taking this to mean the strict sense of cultic sacrifice, we reenact the "spiritual" sacrifice of Saint Paul: making our entire life an offering, by being always open to God who calls us to get beyond ourselves. This does not imply a rejection of worship. There is no love without giving, no giving without some kind of external expression. It is however, the rejection of a certain form of worship which is too closely linked with an outdated religious mentality.

With regard to Jesus Christ, it seems that he can best be considered as the person who reveals man to man. He is the lover who orientates the scattered filings of our diversified desires, the light revealing all our potential which remains hidden within us. The man revealed by Jesus Christ is the person who comes to grips fully with his condition. He is the self-sacrificing man who is prepared for every encounter. He is the man who thinks of another's good before his own. Jesus gives us a model which will haunt the memory of men for all time.

The profound mystery of Christ, in so far as we can get an insight into it, seems to spring forth from the awareness Jesus had of his own mystery. Instead of saying, Jesus is God and man, we say, he is faithful to God (aware of God) and faithful to his human condition (in solidarity with man). The presupposition on which our modern mentality is based was not Sirius' viewpoint about God. There is just one viewpoint, one human interpretation of signs pointing to where God is: Jesus Christ, the sign of signs. But Jesus also joined our search to interpret his own destiny just as the Israelites sought to understand their destiny as a people, and just as each person keeps desiring to understand his own adventure in life through myths, philosophical systems, and artistic creations.

Jesus Christ decided that his destiny would be open to the Absolute. When we proclaim that he is risen, we are saying that his destiny has become the successful model for the rest of us. And we experience in faith (through the Church's testimony and the interior testimony of the Spirit) the life of Jesus Christ which is God's own testimony about life, the divine interpretation of our own human venture.

Through Jesus Christ we know in faith that God speaks, God acts, God loves. Because Jesus kept his entire life open to God, he witnesses to us the awesome effectiveness which such openness brings to a humble human life.

Jesus is likewise considered *the model for the believer.* He is not a philosopher, but listens with his heart; he is not a virtuous aristocrat; he accepts his sinful reputation; he does not lose his sense of direction by being concerned with minute moral principles; he has only one rule—love. This way of identifying Jesus

seems to me to be simple and pregnant with meaning for believers.

Finally, Jesus shows himself to be the sanest man who ever
lived by taking to task the human condition in its twofold nature
of life and death. For him as for us, death seems to hold a cloud
over human existence. Every true human action has two sides:
the side of life and the side of death, because we have to live in
order to die, and we have to die to be alive and to bring life to
others. Jesus is so many things—a solitary because he is a loner,
a martyr because he announces the truth, a sacrifice so that men
might "pass over;" he was upset so that humanity might be at
peace, humiliated so that God's holiness would shine forth. We
now interpret his authentic human destiny as holding the key
for the destiny of every human person. Existence is no longer
a rat race between life and death. It is a continual rebirth in life
through dying. Our struggles, our humiliations, our deaths are
illuminated by the light of his Passover. And we will also be
willing to abandon ourselves to the life/death dialectic in Him
who "has seen the hidden face of death."

When we look at the Church, we see the gap between ancient
and modern sensibilities. The very old prefaces for the dedica-
tion of a Church could be celebrated through observing the
Church's hidden glory, while the reality which is here and now
present was overlooked. We can no longer be satisfied with such
triumphalism. We should go in the opposite direction, instead of
letting outward appearances make us practically forget the profound reality of the Church. We should realize that without the
Church, God would simply be a philosophical question, and
Jesus Christ a sympathetic symbol. Jesus would not be regarded
as the one who is alive and risen, the contemporary of all ages.

The Church is a community and a sacrament, where encounter between Christ and people happens, a simple road to God,
but a road which is designed by God's word spoken to men.

Surely the Church is a Church of sinners. Poverty is often
missing, and so is the enthusiasm to serve people, especially
those who are deprived. And sometimes the Church is not avail-
able to searching out people and lacks truly universal openness.

But, after all, why be ashamed of this weak appearance?
The Church is essentially transitory. She contains God's King-

dom, present and future, but the Kingdom is not restricted to the Church. (I am reminded that these phrases are the echo of our sensitivity and not the proclamation of timeless truths.)

The true richness of the Church, its inalienable dignity, is found in what it has received from the Spirit, the Spirit who is the one who teaches us to pray, the Spirit who is the force of reconciliation and renewal, the Spirit who urges us forward as envoys enlightening and inspiring the world, the Spirit who consecrates bread and wine into Christ's body and blood and forms the human race into the Body of Christ.

For us, the Christian's place is in the world. And this does not mean we have attitudes of superiority, Christians are not any more capable than anyone else to set high standards for others ("I am going to point out to you the absolute epitome of values."), nor is there room for moral taskmasters ("I will tell you what you must do.") Not at all. We are as free as anyone else to choose definitive values and make precise commitments. Both people as individuals and society as a whole are so utterly complex that we will gradually discover that every value is ambiguous and that there is a continuing need to make decisions and seek interpretation. There is an almost contradictory dialectic inherent in every situation. What all this means is that the preemptory prophets who used to indicate very smugly the directions we should take are no longer being listened to.

It seems to me that the unique richness found in the Christian is his certitude about "meaning," that is, what is significant and worthwhile. Ricoeur says: "The measure of hope for history lies in the death and Resurrection of Christ: where sin abounds (wherever humanity is menaced, wherever there is nonsense), grace ever more abounds (there an even deeper meaning can be found)."

This meaning which is central to faith is not a matter of possessing ideas, or having visions of the world, or of saying axioms. The real meaning is Jesus, risen from the dead, and this is the meaning we are called upon to proclaim; we proclaim him constantly to ourselves, because the relationship with a person is never in the sphere of making an acquisition, but in the realm of dialogue. (Here we see how the Eucharist is the center of faith because in the Eucharist we are confronted not just with a reading, but with an event in which we participate through the ritual. Without the Eucharist, without sacraments, faith runs the risk of becoming sidetracked into ideology or religious sentiment.)

*   *   *

This is the flavor of our spiritual awareness. We say "our" very modestly because of the modern awareness in which I personally am quite involved in. But is there not a danger in trusting too much in spontaneous reactions? Do we not risk lessening Christ's message by expressing it according to a particular mentality? I mentioned earlier that these prayers are springboards for contemporary eucharistic prayers; here we are dealing with the expression of the central mystery of faith (the symbolic representation of the Easter Mystery); if we use prayers such as are found in this book, will this not lead only to a "cultural" liturgy which is merely an amplification of modern man's spontaneous religious desires? Is it not the tendency of the texts to celebrate the struggle to achieve human brotherhood, with a slight hint of the gospels?

This is a danger and I admit it. If through discontent with ancient prayers, there is an attempt to create completely new prayers by using the lived experiences of Christian communities, then there is a danger. But is there not a danger too that we might become stale by praying only traditional formulas?

Although these dangers are real, I believe they can be avoided. The first thing we have to do is to be truly open to *all* forms of modern "religious" sentiment. This does not mean that our goal is to form an impossible synthesis, but rather that we are avoiding the error of making any one form of sensibility an absolute. Some prayers in this book are very much in the style espoused by Oosterhuis. Other prayers unfold in the tonality of the sacred collectivity which spilled out into the streets of Paris in May of 1968. These are the two sacred spheres which our modern film makers exploit so well: the sacredness of the I-Thou relationship, and the sacredness of mobs running toward their destiny. God can be found by trusting in another person and also in speeches made to a crowd. Another way of saying this is that faith in God is nourished by the necessity for us to get truly beyond ourselves into the work which needs to be accomplished. I think that the very fact that these two languages are used in this book actually neutralizes the dangers contained in each emphasis when taken separately (anthropomorphism of intimacy and pantheism of collectivity). These two expressions give a heterogeneous community a better opportunity to become aware of itself. Nevertheless, there are other kinds of modern religious sensitivity which, it may be said, are not honored sufficiently in this book. I wish to mention first that *religiosity* which infiltrates modern scientific thought, such as in the doubts of a Rostand or the denials of the structuralists. By questioning man, his way of life, his past, his roots, his ties with the world, with animality, and with the subconscious, there is true "religious" inquiry. It can even be called contemplative questioning, because the goal of science is not to transform but to understand. This is not intended to be, nor should it be taken as a well constructed apologetic. But the simple statement is often made that scientific and technological effort automatically blossoms into a religious sensitivity which justifies having a specific expression in Christian faith. Titov in his space cabin felt himself obliged to talk against God. He revealed his aggressiveness as he thought of "religion" in terms of conquest, while Pravda celebrated the glory of the cosmonauts by overtly using the Ascension myth. Bormann and his crew read the first chapter of Genesis. They did not read the closing section of *The Divine Milieu:* "Lift up your head, O Jerusalem. . . ." which is clearly based on the sacred collectivity. The sacerdotal version of the Creation narrative in Genesis invites us to contemplate what *is* here and now: "See how all things are beautiful . . ."

Another mentality people express today is *the spirituality of the desert.* Eremitic representations lead us to despise ourselves as we follow this spirituality. It is characterized by flight from the world, running from our responsibilities, schizophrenia, etc. But isn't solitude the structure of our human condition? Isn't that what is at the base of authentic communion, the guarantee of commitment and the ransoming of responsibility? If God is the source of our entire being, then he is able to be reached within our dialogues as well as in our moments of solitude. He is the God of the man alone with himself, who bows down before the mystery of man, who accepts himself in his ambiguity, who admits his limits and seeks his share of happiness, the man who refuses to make things black and white and is able to see two sides to every question. This is the man who is always ready to love, who realizes from experience that it is impossible to be completely in another man's shoes. This man's window is always open, but from a window all that can be said is "Hello." He is the man who grows through dialogue, but who is sometimes more and sometimes less than his dialogue. This is someone whom we must also recognize in ourselves as we make our thanksgiving before God.

And finally Bonhoeffer's intuition of a non-religious God should not exclude in any way the need for God as expressed by a man in distress. The "desire" for God over and beyond the "need" for God are two terms which are in constant dialectic tension rather than being formally opposed. Just as in human love, the "desire" for the other person springs forth continually from the "need" to be complemented by the other. And so it is necessary to accept the need for God who fills a void because from this need will flow the desire for God as Other. The basis for true dialogue in faith is found in the mutual seeking of the other and in mutual respect. This dialectic tension: I need God and I am attracted to God is at the very heart of the mysticism of Saint John of the Cross who describes the nights of the soul as precisely the experience of this inner struggle. Man should not have to be downcast in going toward God. Man just has to present himself with his most pressing needs; true encounter with God will steer him clear of false security (coming to God on one's own terms) and lead him to real faith: "I don't ask God to perform my human task, but I do look to God for direction." Disinterested faith is an attitude, not a legal requirement.

And so a constant dialogue with all forms of contemporary religious outlooks is a sure way to respect the transcendence of the God whom we wish to celebrate. In admitting that several languages are needed to speak about the same God, we are rediscovering the old apophatic mentality of the Fathers of Antioch and Alexandria.

But there is still more to be considered. The God we celebrate is not a God who is vaguely present, like gas fumes. *He is the God of Jesus Christ* who has become involved with the material world and its history. The same problem of interpretation confronts contemporary catechists and modern liturgists alike. In this struggle for understanding, we should remember that Christianity is not a religion based on a book. Christianity is belief in an event: the Incarnation and Passover of Jesus Christ. Modern exegesis has taught us to regard the New Testament as an expression of how the first Christian community witnessed this event. This witness is expressed in the categories of representation, expressive myths and forms of religiosity which are no longer our own. We have to reinterpret the Good News of Jesus Christ in our own categories, according to our own myths and religiosity. ("Kerygma" in a pure state does not really exist.) Does this mean that we can no longer use the New Testament? The New Testament remains the "model" for every reinterpretation of the Christ event. Here is what I mean. Anyone who reads the New Testament is soon aware of the very different stresses that are given to some Christian mystery: Paul and James on faith and good works, the Apocalypse and Saint John's gospel on eschatology (man's final destiny), the letters to the Christians at Corinth and the pastoral letters on the internal structure of the Church. These tensions are worthwhile and healthy because they show that the Christian mystery transcends every verbal and notional representation, and that this mystery can be "grasped" only through the synthesis of opposing ideas, sentiments, behavioral patterns and ritual expressions. The New Testament is therefore a model for all subsequent reinterpretation. Each succeeding generation must rediscover, in their own way, the manner in which the Christian experience of that particular era is expressed, along with the same healthy tensions which guarantee the transcendence of the mystery of faith. The community *lives* the mystery of faith in its totality. The community cannot be *aware* of its totality by using one expression exclusively.

Father Jossua applies this same reasoning to the reinterpretation of dogma. He cites Karl Rahner, for example. This theologian attempts to reinterpret traditional christology in terms of existential philosophy and yet is continually on his guard to uphold the Chalcedan formulas as the model for the tensions which must balance out every expression of the mystery of Christ.

Let us apply the above approach to the eucharistic prayer which is an attempt at expressing the Easter Mystery which the ritual actually represents, i.e., makes present here and now. What occurs first is not the expression (the New Testament), but the rite (the event). It is therefore quite normal and even necessary to restate in modern terms the consciousness which the celebrating community has of this rite which makes the salvation event present. I believe that it can be said that we have to create *every piece* of our eucharistic prayers in order to have prayers which are completely modern in expression, just as I must create catechetical approaches which are completely modern in expression. And remember that God's Word is also sacramental.

But what purposes do our ancient prayers serve? It is my belief that they can be compared to the role the New Testament and dogmatic definitions play in catechesis and theology. Ancient prayers are models for every re-expression in the sense of furnishing us with a structure, and indeed a dynamic structure (by combining forces) which we should have in every eucharistic prayer, or more exactly, in every eucharistic prayer celebrated in a home.

The structure of the old type of prayer is easily identified: praise—thanksgiving—institution—anamnesis—offering—epiclesis (intercessions). This structure was never completely rigid. There were additions and stresses. Sometimes very diversified prayers linked one part of the liturgy to the other. But the prayer was set, and this is what provided the organic link with the rite itself. This became the classic model for teaching and living out the eucharistic mystery. Let us restate this more actively by using verbs: to celebrate the Eucharist means to give God strong praise for his own sake (divine praise)—to acknowledge his presence in history (thanksgiving)—to recall what Jesus did (institution—anamnesis)—to offer and be offered—to invoke God's activity. Let us note that there is a dynamic tension involved in these different aspects: to praise (God is Other) and to give thanks (God has intervened in our history), to remember (the supreme gift of Jesus Christ and his Passover), and to offer/be offered (to experience the Passover now and to give of ourselves now), to invoke the Spirit on our gifts (sacramental epiclesis which has for its purpose the consecration of the bread and wine), and to invoke the Spirit in our lives and in the world (communion epiclesis for the consecration of the world).

I believe I can say that I have found an expression of this dynamic equilibrium in the collection of prayers by Jean-Thierry Maertens and Marguerite De Bilde, and that is why the prayers seem to me to be "radically" traditional. After becoming familiar with these prayers, I was convinced that new things can be formed from old models, not by rigid application, but through living assimilation, just like a son is an expression of his father when he develops into adulthood. "Chip off the old block" is a great expression because it stresses both the continuity between the old and the new and their distinction.

We can see this happen to living things, like a child or a tree. Roots deeply buried in the soil, new foliage ready to grasp for the sky. A tree, symbol of life, symbol of prayer. Prayer is nourished in the sap of religious sentiment and reaches toward the sun of faith. Prayer does not tear itself away from the roots of salvation events, but unfolds in the overflowing richness of the diversified expression of this same salvation.

The prayers of Jean-Thierry Maertens, I believe, are a beautiful tree.

A tree which demands a forest around it.